Leeds Trinity
University College

Games, Ideas and Activities for Primary Music

Games, Ideas
and **Activities** for
Primary Music

Donna Minto

Longman
is an imprint of

Harlow, England • London • New York • Boston • San Francisco • Toronto
Sydney • Tokyo • Singapore • Hong Kong • Seoul • Taipei • New Delhi
Cape Town • Madrid • Mexico City • Amsterdam • Munich • Paris • Milan

PEARSON EDUCATION LIMITED
Edinburgh Gate
Harlow CM20 2JE
United Kingdom
Tel: +44 (0)1279 623623
Fax: +44 (0)1279 431059
website: www.pearsoned.co.uk

First edition published in Great Britain in 2009

© Pearson Education Limited 2009

The right of Donna Minto to be identified as author of this work has been asserted
by her in accordance with the Copyright, Designs and Patents Act 1988.

ISBN: 978-1-4082-2326-0

British Library Cataloguing in Publication Data
A CIP catalogue record for this book can be obtained from the British Library

Library of Congress Cataloging in Publication Data
A CIP catalog record for this book can be obtained from the Library of Congress

10 9 8 7 6 5 4 3 2 1
13 12 11 10 09

Set by 30
Printed and bound in Great Britain by Ashford Colour Press Ltd, Gosport, Hants

The Publisher's policy is to use paper manufactured from sustainable forests.

Contents

Introduction   vii

Chapter 1 – Singing   3

Introduction   4

Come and Meet the Solfa
Family   5
Up or Down   10
'The Wild Man from Kettle-O'   12
'Miss Minto Says'   14
'Last Thing at Night'   16
'Stars'   18
'Mousie All Alone'   20
'Clowns' Noses'   22
'Charlie Over the Ocean'   24
Bopping with Bonnie   26
Singing 'Structions   28
Alphabet Antics   30
Beautiful Bubbles   32
Lasso that Sound   34
'Who Can it Be?'   36
Let's See Some Emotion!   38
Singing Jigsaws   40
'We are the Body Band'   42
The Lost Pet   44
Times Tables   47
So–Me Questions and Answers   51
Wacky Words   53
One Word at a Time   54
The Human Scale   55

Advanced   57

'Red Riding Hood'   58
'We've Got a House for You'   62
Super Scales   65
Solfa School Uniform   66

'Name that Tune!'   69
'Body Solfa'   71

Chapter 2 – Playing   75

'Hickory Dickory Dock'   78
'Grand Old Duke of York'   80
Leap and Jump!   82
Count the Cold   85
Explore and Extend   88
Instrument Squares   90
Shake that Skeleton   92
Up and Down and Turnabout   95
Cabbage Patch Countdown   98
Bubble Bounce   100
'Ready to Go!'   102
'Pass the Beaters'   105
Investigate the Instruments   107
Sorting Spot   109
Stretch a Sound   111
Arpeggio Fanfares   113
A Weather Picture   115
'Tell Me Another One'   117
'Have you Seen the Leaves?'   119
Play Pentatonic   121
Drastic Droning   123
Think Sharp   125

Advanced   127

Wrap Up that Inspiration   128
1, 3, 5 and Sometimes 7   130
Playing a Round   132
12-Bar Blues   135
'Time for School'   137
'Moving House'   140

Twinkling Tumblers 143
Five-Finger Tunes 145

Chapter 3 – Rhythm 149

Introduction 150

Clap a Rhyme 151
Tell the Time Rhythms 153
Concentration 155
Clap and Stamp and E-Ha! 157
Candle Game 160
Rhythm Banking 162
Be a Square 165
Press Plastic 167
'Drunken Sailor' Drumming 169
Tap it Out and Pass it On 171
Off Beat/On Beat 173
Sounds and Silence 175
Rhythm Around 177
Happy Music 179
Boom Cha Cha 181
Ten Good Men 183
Rhythm Hot Plates 185
Conducting Capers 187
Rhythm Ostinati 189
Slap, Clap, Say your Word 191
Match the Rhythm 193
'Ugly Bug Ball' 195
3, 4 and 5 197

Advanced 199

Beat Box Body 200
'Digestive System Rap' 202
Frozen Food 205
Taste and Hear the Difference 208
Duet or Trio 210
Rhythm Rondo 212
'The Can Can' 214

Chapter 4 – Listening 217

Introduction 218

High or Low 219
'Teddy Bears' Picnic' 221
Shake and Shoogle 223
Fire-Bell Polka 225
Pat, Pat, Patterns 228
Hide and Seek Sounds 230
Fantastic Four 232
Hup 2, 3, 4 234
Sounds Around 236
'Thunder and Lightning Polka' 238
Classroom Rumble 240
'Pennsylvania 6–5000' 242
'The Syncopated Clock' 244
Instrumental Sets 246
Loud or Quiet 248
How Many Sounds? 250
Good Sound/Bad Sound 252
Stand Up/Sit Down 253

Advanced 255

Up and Down or Left and Right 256
'Alexander's Ragtime Band' 259
'Zabadak' 262
Oom Pah Pah 264
Sleigh Ride 266
'The Little Train of Caipira' 268
Shopping for Sounds 270
Entertain the Entertainer 272
River Runs Red 274
'Alla Turca' Animals 278
Sing the Note then Find It 281
Gallery of Sounds 283

Glossary 285

Appendices 290

Instruments of the orchestra 292
Sources for songs 294

Introduction

'There is no complete personality without music.' Zoltan Kodaly

'Music is too precise to express in words.' Felix Mendelssohn

Purpose

The games and activities in this book are a collection that I have amassed over many years. A lot of the activities have come about as a result of my own teaching in primary schools over the last 30 years. A considerable number of the games I have been fortunate enough to be told about by colleagues or presenters at conferences, have read about or have had in-service day presentations including them. I am very grateful to the many people who have in fact contributed to this book by virtue of the fact they have taught me the activities or given me the ideas.

Hopefully this book will be useful to all primary teachers as a resource to be dipped into when they require an idea for a music lesson. I have tried to present the games in an as user-friendly way as possible. Most of the games can be taught simply and then expanded on if desired. More and more class teachers are finding themselves in the position of being asked to teach music and struggle to find resources and ideas. Hopefully, this book will be useful for doing just that.

How to use this book

The activities are divided into four groups: Singing
Playing
Rhythm
Listening

For each activity, the main focus will be whichever section that activity is in. However, most of the activities cover more than one area and may be used for any of the four section headings – some cover all four! In all music activities, the emphasis should be on enjoyment. At the end of each activity there are suggested cross-curricular links and I am sure the class teacher will be able to think of many more.

Each section is arranged with activities most suited to Key Stage 1 first (KS1), followed by those for all ages (KS1 and KS2) and finally those best for Key Stage 2 (KS2). At the end of each section are activities labelled 'Advanced' which are probably best tackled after trying a few of the earlier activities. These classifications are only meant to be a general guide. It is possible to adapt any of the ideas to suit other age groups. Each activity includes variations which give ideas for differentiating the activity from its original version. Key Stage 2 teachers will find lots of useful ideas in the Key Stage 1 activities and vice versa. There is a Music Glossary appendix where the meaning of words in bold type can be found.

Notable Songs Limited

Most of the songs used in this book are written by Donna Minto and are available in 25 topic-related packs from: Notable Songs Ltd
5 Kingswood Grove
Kingswells
Aberdeen
AB15 8AH
www.notablesongs.co.uk

This company was started to overcome the enormous copyright difficulties that frequently exist with regard to the photocopying of music. Each song from Notable Songs Ltd can be photocopied freely by the purchaser. The purpose in including these songs in this book was to overcome any copyright issues which could have arisen in using material written by anyone else. All the songs – and numerous other material produced by Donna Minto – used in this book can be viewed/downloaded from the companion website at www.pearsoned.co.uk/minto.

Musical instruments

A lot of the activities, particularly in the playing and rhythmic sections, require some musical instruments. Obviously, the provision in each school varies enormously but I have assumed that there are some basic requirements as far as the provision of musical instruments is concerned. In the appendices, there is a list of the many possibilities for classroom percussion.

When writing the activities I have assumed that for a class of 30 children there will ideally be a minimum of 15 chromatic (with sharps and flats) tuned percussion instruments (glockenspiels and xylophones). Each child requires two matching beaters, i.e. 60 beaters. The need for two beaters is to facilitate the use of alternate beaters when playing on these instruments. Obviously, it is possible for two children sharing an instrument to take turn about so that each has two beaters when it is their turn to play.

I have also assumed a minimum provision of 8–10 tambourines, triangles, tambours, woodblocks, guiros, pairs of rhythm sticks, sleigh bells, maracas,

Indian bells, cymbals and handled castanets. The possibilities are endless and usually quite expensive but it is folly to expect to be able to teach music without providing a basic minimum of the classroom instruments required. The best possible scenario is for there to be a tuned, chromatic percussion instrument with two matching beaters for each child and it is always worth having that as a goal to work towards.

Basic ground rules for musical activities

Music is a mental discipline and as such students require clear guidelines as to the type of behaviour expected during a music lesson. The following suggestions for ground rules will allow the students to obtain maximum benefit and enjoyment from their musical activities:

> Only touch the musical instruments when asked.
> Leave the beaters on top of the instrument when not in use.
> Do not play when you are meant to be listening.
> Treat the instruments with respect.
> Look when you are listening.

There is an appendix which gives many suggestions for the types of classroom percussion instruments that are available.

The following music statement gives an idea of the enormous effect that involvement in musical activities can have on a child's ability to learn.

MUSIC

Music education is more than learning to sing or play an instrument.
It is more than entertaining or pleasing an audience.
It is more than a pleasant diversion or recreation.

Music is a science, a mental discipline, and an art.
It has a mathematical foundation; it is a language and physical activity.

Any subject that combines science, discipline, language, maths, physical activity and art must not only be worthwhile but absolutely essential to the education of our children.

Music incorporates every other area of study in some way.

Acknowledgements

A hugh thank you to Ken, Jenny, Carrie, Ross and Rachel for their perseverance and patience! I would also like to thank the pupils and staffs of the schools I teach in for allowing me to experiment on them!

To my parents – Jean and Allan – who instilled in me the need to work hard in order to be able to follow my dreams.

Chapter 1
Singing

Introduction

'I can only think of music as something inherent in every human being – a birthright. Music coordinates mind, body and spirit. That doesn't mean that each person must have a violin or piano: the greatest service to the population would be if every school day could begin with singing. If they sing together they have a feeling of each individual in his or her own coordination as well as each within the body of the group. I have never met a member of a choir who was depressed.' Yehudi Menuhin

Singing is, and always should be, an enjoyable, uplifting and non-threatening activity. In the following activities there is a full range of song types including 'fun' songs, part singing, solo singing and also solfa work. The first activity introduces the solfa scale and several of the other singing activities refer to it. The solfa system is an invaluable tool for the teaching of singing and also notation.

It is extremely important when encouraging children to sing individually that the whole atmosphere in which this is done is encouraging and non-judgemental. Someone can be inhibited from singing for life by a critical look or reaction to their contribution. When sharing their singing voice with others in a group, a child is opening themselves up to a considerable degree and it is vital that clear ground rules are set for everyone. The most vital rule being that everyone's contribution is valued and appreciated.

Equally, if a child chooses not to sing, treat that choice with respect – silence is a vital part of any music making. It is so important that singing games are not threatening in any way but relaxed and fun. A child will still be able to participate with the whole group even though they don't feel confident enough to sing alone.

The last six activities in this section are advanced.

Come and Meet the Solfa Family

Suitable for

KS1, KS2

Aims

- To understand ascending and descending, high and low concepts.
- To introduce a scale – eight notes stepping up or down.
- To introduce **solfa** names.

Resources

- A3 size copy of the **solfa staircase** (see pp. 7–8) with eight named people – one on each step of the staircase
- Ideally this should be laminated so that the people can be taken on and off the steps
- Tuned percussion instrument – glockenspiel or xylophone
- Alternatively, a piano or keyboard

What to do

- Have the solfa staircase where everyone can see it and ask the children to tell you what they can see:
  - Lots of different-coloured children on a staircase
  - Red boy **doe** is at the bottom of the stairs
  - Purple girl doe is at the top of the stairs, i.e. they have the same name but are quite different in several ways.
- On a glockenspiel (metal bars), xylophone (wooden bars), piano or keyboard, play the notes:

  C   D   E   F   G   A   B   C

- Starting on **middle C** (so called because it is in the middle of the piano keyboard), middle C on a classroom **glockenspiel** or **xylophone** is the large size C bar.
- You are playing the staircase from bottom to top.
- Red doe is played on middle C so play C   C   C whilst singing
  doe   doe   doe

- The class can then sing doe   doe   doe back to you.
- Repeat this going all the way up the staircase:
  red doe = C
  green ray = D
  orange me = E
  pink fa = F
  blue so = G
  yellow la = A
  brown tee = B
  purple doe = C.
- Ask the children if they can hear that the notes they are singing go up the stairs i.e. get higher – fancy word for that is **ascending**.
- Repeat the exercise but this time start on the C for purple doe and go down the stairs – fancy word for this is **descending**.
- Play red doe C then purple doe C singing doe   doe   doe each time – the class are then singing low doe followed by high doe and can easily connect the high/low concept with what they have visually in front of them.

Variations

- The possibilities are endless.
- You can sing little snippets like doe, ray, me OR me, ray, doe.
- Doe, me, doe OR me, fa, so OR so, me, so ...
- You could write the notes C   D   E   F   G   A   B   C   in their appropriate colours and the children could compose their own little songs, e.g.

  Doe, doe, doe, doe, ray, me.
  Me, me, me, me, ray, doe.

- With younger children you could restrict the number of notes – start with only red doe then over a number of weeks, introduce each note.
- You could have several sets of the solfa people cards and the children can 'write' their own song to sing using the solfa people pictures as their music.

Cross-curricular links

Letters – capital sounds or initial sounds for infants.
Colours – connecting colour to appropriate person and name.
Language – ascending, descending, high, low, stepping.
Maths – up one, down one, jump a space, eight notes up, eight notes down.
PSHE – we're all different but can work together.

* Images available to download from the website

Up or Down

Suitable for

KS1

Aims

- To introduce the concept of **intervals** using the solfa staircase (see pp. 7, 8, 9).
- To allow the children freedom to experiment with their voices using only three notes.
- To encourage familiarity with the first three notes of the solfa scale.

Resources

- A laminated copy of the solfa staircase and each of the people on it
- A **tuned percussion** instrument with only low C, D and E bars on it

What to do

- Have the solfa staircase where everyone can see it and have only doe (at the bottom of the staircase), ray and me in position on the staircase.
- The leader of this activity should play C, D, E on the tuned percussion instrument and ask the children to sing the notes back to the names doe, ray, me.
- The leader should then play as many different variations as possible and tell the children what names they should sing back, e.g.

  E, D, C = me, ray, doe
  D, D, C = ray, ray, doe
  C, E, C = doe, me, doe
  E, E, C = me, me, doe

- Once the children are confident at singing the melodies back with the solfa names, the leader should explain that from now on, the notes will be played but the children have to guess what the solfa names are.
- The leader plays a three-note tune and asks an individual to guess/ work out what the solfa names are, e.g. C, C, D = doe, doe, ray.
- If the child answers correctly, then everyone in the class sings the solfa names back to the leader and another tune is played for guessing.

Variation

- When a child correctly works out the solfa name, that child could then play a three-note tune and whoever guesses it correctly, gets to play the next tune.

Cross·curricular links

Language – listening, auditory discrimination, memory and recall.
Maths – awareness of patterns, vocabulary of up, down, stays the same, positional awareness.
PSHE – cooperation, taking a turn, sharing, concentration.

'The Wild Man from Kettle-O'

Suitable for

KS1

Aims

- To enable the children to sing an accumulative song using drama as an aid.
- To encourage the enjoyment of telling a story through song.

Resources

- A recording of 'The Wild Man from Kettle-O' by The Singing Kettle Group – it is on *Singing Kettle* CD No.3
- A CD player
- Optional costumes or masks for each of the characters mentioned in the song:
  - The wild man from Kettle-O
  - The wife
  - The daughter
  - The husband
  - The son
  - The big, black, fluffy dog
  - The pale, blue budgie
  - The titchy, itchy, scritchy, scratchy flea

What to do

- Organise the children to act out the characters mentioned in the song. It is possible to do this without any props, but is a lot of fun if masks, costumes, props are used.
- Let the children first of all listen to the recording and simply stand up as their character is mentioned.
- The next time the song is played, ask the first character – the wild man from Kettle-O – to stand every time their name is mentioned and sit down again immediately afterwards.
- Gradually add the other characters and ask them to stand up as their name is mentioned and sit down immediately afterwards.
- By the end of the song it becomes very hectic!
- Everyone should be joining in with the singing as this dramatisation of the song is taking place.

Variation

- When the song is sung over again, ask different children to take the roles of the characters but have them standing/sitting in front of the first cast. Eventually, have every child taking part and three or four of each character.

Cross-curricular links

Drama – the dramatisation of the song, the potential development of the characters.

Topic work – this would fit with a topic about ourselves, families, people who help us.

Language – description of characters, development of a story.

'Miss Minto Says'

Suitable for

KS1

Aims

- To encourage careful listening whilst singing.
- To develop children's coordination in playing or moving whilst singing.

Resources

- Insert the name of the teacher leading the activity in place of 'Miss Minto' in the song 'Miss Minto Says'.
- A selection of untuned percussion instruments.

What to do

- Ask the children to repeat each line of the song after you:

C	FF	F	E	F	G		
Miss	Minto	says	clap	your	hands	X	X
C	GG	G	F	G	A		
Miss	Minto	says	pat	your	knees	X	X
A	Bb Bb	D	Bb	Bb	A G	A G	F
Miss	Minto	says	make	a	funny	buzzing	sound
F	AG	C	D	E	F		
And	become	a	swarm	of	bees!	(bzz	bzz)

- Practise the song until the children are confident in singing and doing the various actions at the correct places.
- Repeat the song but change the actions, e.g.

Miss Minto says click your fingers X X
Miss Minto says tap your toes X X
Miss Minto says make your fingers touch the ground
Walk them right up to your nose.

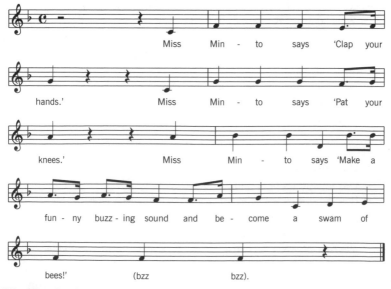

- Another verse could be:

  Miss Minto says pat your head X X
  Miss Minto says pat your chest X X
  Miss Minto says put your thumbs beside your ears
  Make the noise you like the best (squeak, squeak).

- Encourage the children to come up with ideas for other verses.

Variation

- Instead of body percussion use actual percussion instruments:

  Miss Minto says play maraca X X
  Miss Minto says play your drum X X
  Miss Minto says shake your tambourine around
  And you'll have a lot of fun!

Cross-curricular links

PE – coordination and movement.
Language – use of rhyming words and action words, following instructions.

Miss Min - to says 'Clap your

hands.'   Miss   Min - to   says 'Pat your

knees.'   Miss   Min - to   says 'Make a

fun - ny buzz - ing sound and be - come a swam of

bees!'   (bzz   bzz).

'Miss Minto Says' ...

'Last Thing at Night'

Suitable for

KS1

Aims

- To encourage children to sing about everyday activities.
- To develop the use of solfa in singing activities.
- To reinforce stepping notes.

Resources

- A copy and/or recording of the song and someone willing to sing it to the class.
- A copy of the solfa staircase with all the people in their places.

What to do

- Have a discussion about bedtime routines and ask the children what they have to do before they are ready to go to bed.
- Let the children hear the song and ask them about the items that the child needs before going to bed.
- Sing through the first verse and point out when the notes step downwards (before I go to bed) and when they step upwards (rest my sleepy head).
- Ask the children to listen to the notes that are written at the end of the song.
- In solfa these notes are:

  Doe tee la so, doe tee la so, so la tee doe, la tee doe.

- Show the children these notes on the staircase and point out that they all step either upwards or downwards.
- Practise singing the notes using their solfa names – teach them in groups of four notes at a time.
- Once the children know the song and the solfa notes they can alternate between the two as the solfa notes fit together with the tune (like a **descant**).

Variations

- Have soloists for singing the three verses.
- Divide the class into two and have one half singing the song words whilst the other half sing the solfa notes.

Cross-curricular links

Language – discussing routines, repeating words with one line that changes.
Maths – counting in steps or jumps.
PSHE – discussion of what makes us feel secure.

'Last Thing at Night'

'Stars'

Suitable for

KS1

Aims

- To develop the use of stepping notes in singing.
- To encourage careful counting within a song.

Resources

- A copy and/or recording of the song with someone willing to sing the song to the class
- A CD player

What to do

- Have a short discussion about stars and ask the children if they know any star songs – it is likely they will all know 'Twinkle, twinkle' and perhaps 'Star light, star bright'.
- Let the children hear the song and question them about the content, e.g.
  - What is the nearest star to Earth?
  - Does the Sun spin round the Earth or the Earth spin round the Sun?
- Teach the song a **phrase** at a time and ask the children to count the beats in between their singing, e.g.:

  'Twinkling up so high' 1 2 3 4
  'Sparkling in the sky' 1 2 3 4
  'As I stand and stare' 1 2 3 4
  'I ask: How do stars get there?' 1 2

- Once the children are confident at their singing part, add twinkling sounds in the spaces using triangle, Indian bells and glockenspiels. The children must count carefully to play only the number of beats after each phrase.

Variation

- For older or more able children, they could work out the note names of the **melody** in between phrases and play these notes on a glockenspiel after each phrase is sung.

Cross-curricular links

Science – the night sky, earth and sun, space.
Maths – counting and noticing patterns.
Language – remembering a phrase and pausing before the next phrase.

'Stars Song'

'Mousie All Alone'

Suitable for

KS1

Aims

- To encourage the class to sing as a group whilst also holding and passing an instrument.
- To encourage listening with singing.
- To introduce a game which requires singing as a part of it.

Resources

- A selection of percussion instruments
- A leader who knows the song well

What to do

- The class sit in a circle and one person sits in the middle as the mousie.
- Everyone practises singing the song:

C	E	G	high C	A	high C	G
Mousie	sits	there	all	a –		lone

F	G	E	G	G	A	B	high C
Can	he/she	guess	where	the	bells	have	gone?

- The mousie then curls up like a mouse and the class pass a set of sleigh bells around the outside of the circle as quietly as they can whilst singing the song.
- When the song is finished, the mousie has to try and guess where the bells are.
- It may take several singings of the song for the mousie to guess correctly.
- Once the bells have been found, the mousie swaps places with the person who had the bells and the game continues.

Variations

- The instrument being passed can change. Choosing a potentially difficult instrument to pass quietly, e.g. tambourine, rain stick, chime bar and beater makes it more likely that the mousie will be able to guess correctly where the instrument is.
- To take the game a step further, you could have two mousies and two instruments being passed in opposite directions around the outside of the circle – much harder!

Cross·curricular links

PSHE – working together for a common purpose.
Language – honing listening skills.

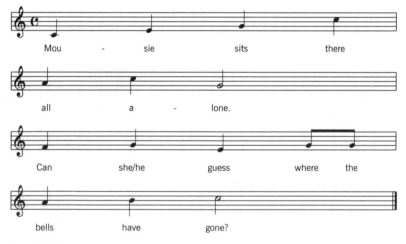

'Mousie All Alone'

'Clowns' Noses'

Suitable for

KS1

Aims

- To use singing in a game to encourage children to recognise the directions the notes are moving in, particularly ascending and descending.
- To develop the recognition of colours.
- To use actions to enhance a song.

Resources

- A poster of several clowns, all with different-coloured noses
- A copy and/or recording of the 'Clowns' Noses' song and someone who is happy to teach it to the class

What to do

- Show the poster and discuss it.
- Sing the song to the children then ask them to join in on the 'Up! Up! Up!' and 'Down! Down! Down!', eventually singing those words and simultaneously moving upwards on 'Up!' and downwards on 'Down!'
- Obtain a few volunteers who are willing to try and point out a specific colour of nose.
- Either, the leader sings the first part of the song and the class join in for the second half or the whole class learn all of the song.
- In the second half of the song, the children move upwards on 'Up!', downwards on 'Down!', they wiggle on 'Wiggle it about'. And they give a funny shout on 'Give a funny shout'.
- At the end of the song, the children do as the words say: 'Turn around and then sit down.'

Variations

- The actual notes for 'Up! Up! Up!' are A B C and the actual notes for 'Down! Down! Down!' are G F E. Some of the class could play these notes on **tuned percussion**, reinforcing the ascending and descending nature of the melody.
- For the very last phrase: 'Turn around and then sit down', the notes required are all descending: B A G F E D C.

Cross-curricular links

Art – reinforcement of colours.
PE – movement in the actions of the song.
Language – functional language, reinforced in the teaching of ascending and descending in music.

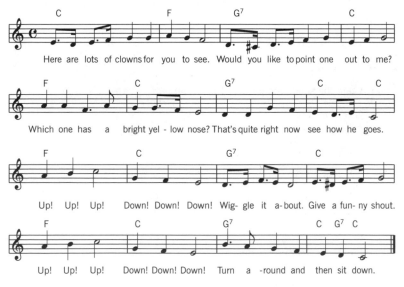

'Clowns' Noses'

'Charlie Over the Ocean'

Suitable for

KS1

Aims

- To encourage singing as part of a group and as a soloist.
- To make singing an enjoyable activity.

Resources

- A copy of the song 'Charlie Over the Ocean'
- Enough room for the children involved to form a circle
- Voices

What to do

- Learn the song 'Charlie Over the Ocean':

G G	G G	G	A B	
Charlie	over	the	ocean	

G G	G G	G	E D	
Charlie	over	the	sea	

G G	G	G	A	B
Charlie	caught	a	big	fish

G	D	G		
Can't	catch	me!		

- The children stand in a circle with 'Charlie' leading the singing whilst walking around the outside of the circle.
- Everyone in the circle echoes each line after Charlie.
- At the last echo, Charlie taps someone on the shoulder and they chase Charlie around the circle then they become Charlie.

Variation

- To give those children who would rather not sing on their own a get-out clause, say that the person who is tapped on the shoulder can chase Charlie, but can choose whether or not they become Charlie. If they like they can designate who they want to be Charlie or, alternatively, they could ask for volunteers.

It's important to make the game non-threatening for those children who feel less confident at singing by themselves.

Cross-curricular links

PSHE – confidence building, being part of a group but also having the opportunity to work alone.
PE – movement, running, chasing.

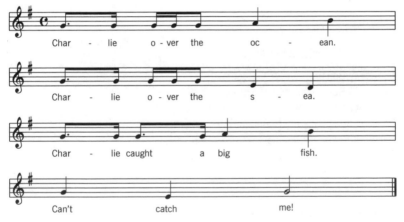

'Charlie Over the Ocean'

Bopping with Bonnie

Suitable for

KS1, KS2

Aims

- To encourage full participation in singing a song.
- To combine action with voice.
- To encourage anticipation and thinking skills.

Resources

- Ideally done with everyone sitting on a chair

What to do

- Practise singing the whole song:

  My Bonnie lies over the ocean
  My Bonnie lies over the sea
  My Bonnie lies over the ocean
  O bring back my Bonnie to me
  Bring back, bring back
  O bring back my Bonnie to me, to me
  Bring back, bring back
  O bring back my Bonnie to me.

- Ask the children to stand up on the first 'Bonnie' then sit down on the next 'Bonnie' and continue until the song is finished (they should end up sitting).
- Sing the song again but this time stand up or sit down on any word beginning with 'B' (they should still end up sitting but having moved many more times on 'Bonnie', 'bring' and 'back').

Variation

- Divide the class into two groups. One group do the song moving only on 'Bonnie' whilst the other group move on words beginning with 'B'.

Cross-curricular links

Topic work – fits in with any study of Scotland.
Maths – up and down; patterns.
Language – initial letters.

Singing 'Structions

Suitable for

KS1, KS2

Aims

- To encourage singing as an everyday activity.
- To calm the class through singing.
- To increase listening skills through singing.

Resources

- A teacher willing to sing unaccompanied!

What to do

- As part of the everyday routine, sing out instructions to your class and ask the class to echo your instructions (singing) when they hear them, e.g.

Teacher	Class
Put away your paper	Put away our paper
Line up at the door	Line up at the door
Do it very quietly	Doing it very quietly
Listen as you go	Listening as we go

- Any instruction is best sung using only two or three different notes e.g.

Put	away	your	pa-	per
G	GE	A	G	E

- The three notes A, G and E are ideal as they are in a good range for primary school children.

Variations

- Ask a child to be the singing leader for the day.
- Do all your one-to-one questioning in this manner!

Cross·curricular links

Topic work – have mini quizzes with information about a topic being studied. Sing the questions and ask the answerer to sing back the answer.

PSHE – confidence building, team building (whole class responds together).

Alphabet Antics

Suitable for

KS1, KS2

Aims

- To make up nonsense rhymes using a letter from the alphabet.
- To sing these rhymes to a partner and then combine two rhymes to make a song with two sections, e.g. A, B, A.

Resources

- Willing voices

What to do

- In pairs, the children choose a letter of the alphabet, e.g. 'M'.
- Individually each child makes up a nonsense rhyme, e.g.

  meme me, mosa, ma
  Minnie mousie maxi.

- Using only two or three notes – E, G and A – the game starts with the song:

This	is	a	song	about	'M' –	What's	that	you	say?
G	G	G	E	EA	GE	G	G	A	GE

- The first child then sings their nonsense rhyme using the same three notes:

Me	me	me	mo –	sa	ma	
G	G	E	G	A	E	(This part of the song is section A)

- The second child then sings their nonsense rhyme using the same three notes:

Min –	nie	mou –	sie	ma –	xi	
A	G	A	G	E	E	(This part of the song is section B)

- The pair then experiment with how they want their song to be constructed, e.g., it could be ABA or AABB or AABA or any variation they wanted.
- As a pair they perform their song about the letter 'M'.

Variations

- The number of notes to be used in the composing could be increased.
- The song needn't have a letter as its subject matter; any topic being studied would work just as well.

Cross-curricular links

Language – initial letters, poetry, alliteration, construction of a song.

Maths – problem solving – in pairs, constructing a song using two sections and deciding on the pattern each pair uses.

Topic work – making up songs/rhymes about a topic under study.

Beautiful Bubbles

Suitable for

KS1, KS2

Aims

- To encourage experimentation in the use of the voice.
- To add an appropriate accompaniment to a song.

Resources

- A recording of the song 'I'm Forever Blowing Bubbles' by Jaan Kenbrovin and John William Kellette
- A tub of bubbles and wand
- Willing voices

What to do

- Learn the song:

  I'm forever blowing bubbles
  Pretty bubbles in the air
  They fly so high
  Nearly reach the sky
  Then like my dreams they fade and die
  Fortune's always hiding
  I've looked everywhere
  I'm forever blowing bubbles
  Pretty bubbles in the air.

- Once the song is secure, ask the children to make beautiful bubble music by singing 'oooh' at different pitches (notes). It will take a bit of practice to achieve the appropriate gentleness of sound.
- The teacher then asks the class to watch while bubbles are blown.
- Next they choose one bubble to watch until it reaches the ground and eventually bursts.
- The next stage is to vocalise whilst following their bubble and make a 'p' sound when it bursts.
- Once this has been practised a few times, the class vocalisation will make an unusual **coda** (ending) to the song which will be different every time.

Variation

- Each child could try and vary the pitch of their bubble note according to the direction the bubble moves in, i.e.

```
        O
     O     O
  O        O
           O
              O
                'p'
```

Cross-curricular links

Science – what do the bubbles do? Is it predictable? How is sound produced?
Language – use of different sounds with the voice.

Lasso that Sound

Suitable for

KS1, KS2

Aims

- To encourage an understanding of how the voice moves.
- To help children to hear their voice moving.

Resources

- A long piece of rope – like a skipping rope for many people
- People to hold and manipulate the rope

What to do

- The rope is held taut and level.
- The leader 'sings' the rope by choosing one **pitch** and singing whilst moving a hand along the rope.
- The class are asked to join in. The main aim is to sustain one sound so the accuracy of the pitch of each individual note is not important.
- Next the rope is allowed to sag in the centre so that an arc is formed.
- Still with a hand moving along the rope, the leader sings from a reasonably high sound, sliding down to a low sound then sliding back up to the starting point.
- The physical action of moving along the rope helps to reinforce what is happening with the voice.
- The rope is then held up in the middle and the sound starts low and climbs up and then down again.

Variations

- With more people manipulating the rope, a more complex melody can be produced.
- Alternatively, the class can be divided into two groups and they sing simultaneously with one group starting at the opposite end of the rope to the other group.

Cross·curricular links

Science – voice production/sound production.
PSHE – working as part of a team.

'Who Can it Be?'

Suitable for

KS1, KS2

Aims

- To encourage **improvisation** in singing.
- To make solo singing non-threatening.

Resources

- A blindfold
- A song using the notes E, G and A, e.g.

G G	E	A	G E	A	G	E
Susan's	in	the	middle,	she	can't	see

G G	E A	G G E	G	G	G	E
Listen	very	carefully,	who	can	it	be?

What to do

- All the children sit in a circle and one is chosen to be blindfolded standing in the centre.
- The circle of children sings the song.
- The leader sings a question to a child in the circle using the notes G and E, e.g.

G	G	G	E
Are	you	a	boy?

- The child being asked the question sings his reply:

G	G	E
Yes	I	am

- The child in the middle has to try and guess who sang the reply.
- If they guess correctly then they swap places and the game continues.
- If the person in the centre cannot guess or guesses wrongly, the leader can keep singing questions to try and help.

It is extremely important that no criticism is made of the person singing the reply. Someone can be inhibited from singing for life by a critical look or reaction to their contribution. Equally, if a child chooses not to sing, treat that choice with respect – silence is a vital part of any music making. It is so important that singing games are not threatening in any way but relaxed and fun. A child will still be able to participate with the whole group even though they don't feel confident enough to sing alone.

Variation

- If the children around the circle are feeling confident enough, it is possible to dispense with the leader asking questions and just get the person to be guessed to sing something for the child in the middle to listen to, e.g.

G	G	G	E	A	G G	G	E
Who	do	you	think	is	singing	to	you?

Cross-curricular links

Language – question and answer, confident use of language.
PSHE – confidence building, being part of a team and an individual.

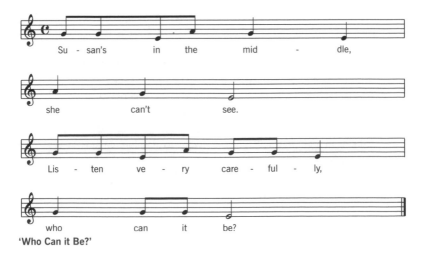

'Who Can it Be?'

Let's See Some Emotion!

Suitable for

KS1, KS2

Aims

- To encourage singing for enjoyment.
- To develop the use of emotion in singing.

Resources

- A few ideas of songs that the children will know well, e.g.

  'Happy Birthday',
  'Head, Shoulders, Knees and Toes',
  'If You're Happy and You Know It',
  'The Wheels on the Bus'.

What to do

- Sing the song normally.
- Sing the song but in a chosen emotion e.g. sadly, angrily, happily, poshly, etc.
- Do this a few times with different emotions and ask the children to really go for it with facial expressions and body language.
- Next ask the children to sing the song happily with all the necessary expression then change the emotion but the voice has to stay happy, e.g., have an angry expression but sing in a happy voice or have a sad expression but sing in a happy voice.
- This is really difficult to do and will take quite a bit of practice!
- Obviously, the two different emotions can change, e.g., have a happy expression but sing in a sad voice, have a happy expression but sing in a grumpy voice, have a happy expression but sing in a bored voice.

Variations

- Make a list of emotions then match two for the game.
- Discover which emotions are easy to fake and which are virtually impossible.

Cross-curricular links

Drama – showing emotion facially and with your body language.
Language – listing emotions and turning them into adjectives.
PSHE – how we show what we are feeling and what that should tell other people about us and how to react to us.

Singing Jigsaws

Suitable for

KS1, KS2

Aims

- To encourage children to 'feel' the **beat** by internalising it during singing.
- To develop the children's ability to keep a song or melody going in their head.

Resources

- A selection of well-known songs and/or songs that the children are familiar with, e.g.
  'Head, Shoulders, Knees and Toes'
  'If You're Happy and You Know It Clap Your Hands'
  'Ten Green Bottles'
  'The Grand Old Duke of York'
  'My Bonnie Lies Over the Ocean'
  'The Hokey Cokey'

What to do

- Ask the class to sing the chosen song whilst tapping the beat on their knees.
- Once everyone is sure of the words and melody, sing the song again with the tapping but this time do every second line singing the song in your head but continuing to tap the beat on your knees.
- With the help of the tapping, everyone should come in correctly after the silent line.
- Next try missing out every second word but still keep tapping on your knees.
- It is sometimes easier to do this if the words are displayed on a screen or board with every second word underlined.
- Finally, try the missing line then missing every second word without the aid of the tapping to keep the beat and speed steady. This is much harder!

Variation

- Choose a song the children have been learning as part of their Environmental Studies topic.

Cross-curricular links

Language – sorting out and correct placing of words in songs and poems.
Maths – counting beats, finding the correct place and time to come in with the next line.

'We are the Body Band'

Suitable for

KS1, KS2

Aims

- To encourage singing with rhythmic accompaniment.
- To develop physical coordination and fluency.
- To develop intelligent listening whilst singing.

Resources

- Lots of bodies with voices!

What to do

- Teach the children the song:

G	G	A	G F	E		
We	are	the	body	band		

D D	G	F	E	G	D	
Listen	to	us,	we're	so	grand	

G	G	G	A	G	F	E
Hear	us	as	we	stamp	our	feet

D	D	G	F	E	D	C
One,	two,	three,	a	nice	strong	beat.

- Add more verses with appropriate words, e.g. only the last two lines need to be changed for clapping hands, patting cheeks, clicking fingers, etc.

  Hear us as we clap our hands
  We're the best in all the land.

  Hear us as we pat our cheeks
  They're bright red from patting all week!

  Hear us as our fingers click
  We're so good we never miss a trick.

Variations

- Once the children can perform the verses confidently, try missing out the words in the last line but just put in the body sound, e.g., stamping. Make sure this is done with the correct rhythm according to what the words are.
- If the children feel confident doing that then the class could be divided into several groups who all sing the same first two lines then divide into whatever body band sound they have been allocated and have several different parts playing together at the end of the song.

Cross-curricular links

PE – encouraging coordination and physical fluency of movement.
Language – rhyming words, rhythmic patterns of word.
PSHE – working as part of a team, relying on others to keep a part going.

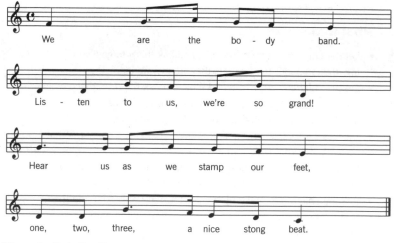

'**We are the Body Band**'

The Lost Pet

Suitable for

KS1, KS2

Aims

- To encourage the children to use singing for relaying information.
- To develop the children's ability to make up more words for a song.

Resources

- A copy and/or recording of the song 'My Cat is Lost – Oh No!'
- A CD player
- A copy of the 'Lost' poster

What to do

- Let the children listen to the song and ask them to give you information about the animals that are mentioned.
- Let the children listen a second time and ask them to notice which parts of the song use the same words in both verses.
- Let the children try singing along with the recording.
- Discuss each verse as you sing it, e.g. What is the animal? What colour is it? What is its name?
- Once both verses have been rehearsed and discussed, ask the children if they can think of another pet that might go missing.
- Ask the children to make up a verse for that pet but remind them that a lot of the words stay the same with only the name, colour and type of animal to fill in.
- Perform the song with the given verses and any that the class make up.

Variation

- Get the children to use the 'Lost' poster to illustrate the verse they have produced for the song.

Cross-curricular links

Art – poster stimulus comes from the song.
Language – choosing appropriate language for describing the lost pet.
    – making up words for the other verse of the song – scanning, syllables.
    – comprehension – gleaning information from each verse of the song.

LOST

Pet's name: _____

Description: _____

_____

Last seen: _____

If spotted please contact: _____

_____

at: _____

'My Cat is Lost – Oh No!'

Times Tables

Suitable for

KS1, KS2

Aims

- To use singing to aid the memorising of times tables.
- To encourage the children to think of rhyming words.

Resources

- A copy and/or recording of the song 'Tables Song'
- A CD player

What to do

- Go over the particular times table you would like to start practising with the children.
- Let the children hear the verse of the song that covers that particular times table.
- Let the children listen again and they can put in the answers only to each stage of the table.
- Let the children learn the introductory words:

  When you're counting numbers, sing this little song
  Then you'll know your tables. Then you won't go wrong. Let's Go!

- Encourage the children to sing the 'Let's Go!' with lots of enthusiasm.
- At the end of the table ask the children to point out the word that rhymes with the last calculation.
- Ask the children if they are happy with that word or if they have a better rhyming word to insert there.
- Choose one, some or all of the tables to practise using this song.

Variations

- The four-note descending part could be sung and/or played between each times table. If wished these four notes could be sung to their solfa names of doe, tee, la, so.
- During the singing of the times table, the class could be divided into two halves and one half sing the question whilst the other half sing the answer.

Cross-curricular links

Maths – times tables practice.

Language – recognising and improvising with rhyming words.

'Tables Song'

6 × 0 = 0	7 × 0 = 0	8 × 0 = 0
6 × 1 = 6	7 × 1 = 7	8 × 1 = 8
6 × 2 = 12	7 × 2 = 14	8 × 2 = 16
6 × 3 = 18	7 × 3 = 21	8 × 3 = 24
6 × 4 = 24	7 × 4 = 28	8 × 4 = 32
6 × 5 = 30	7 × 5 = 35	8 × 5 = 40
6 × 6 = 36	7 × 6 = 42	8 × 6 = 48
6 × 7 = 42	7 × 7 = 49	8 × 7 = 56
6 × 8 = 48	7 × 8 = 56	8 × 8 = 64
6 × 9 = 54	7 × 9 = 63	8 × 9 = 72
6 × 10 = 60	7 × 10 = 70	8 × 10 = 80
A dog called Pixie	Our tummies are empty!	Aye, aye, matey!

9 × 0 = 0	10 × 0 = 0
9 × 1 = 9	10 × 1 = 10
9 × 2 = 18	10 × 2 = 20
9 × 3 = 27	10 × 3 = 30
9 × 4 = 36	10 × 4 = 40
9 × 5 = 45	10 × 5 = 50
9 × 6 = 54	10 × 6 = 60
9 × 7 = 63	10 × 7 = 70
9 × 8 = 72	10 × 8 = 80
9 × 9 = 81	10 × 9 = 90
9 × 10 = 9	10 × 10 = 100
Can I have another pinty?	None of us have blundered.

So-Me Questions and Answers

Suitable for

KS1, KS2

Aims

- To give children an opportunity to gain confidence in echoing a short phrase.
- To allow children the freedom to choose **solo** or **unison** singing.
- To develop children's listening skills in relation to answering a melodic phrase.

Resources

- The solfa staircase with only so and me placed on the steps
- A selection of questions for asking the children in song

What to do

- Using only the notes so and me (using the notes G and E), the leader of this activity asks the children as a group some simple questions:

  G   G   G   G   G   G   E
  What did you have for breakfast?

  GG   EE   E
  I had Coco Pops.

  G   G   G   E   E
  What is your full name?

  G   G   G   E E
  Donna Jean Minto

  G   G   G   E
  Where do you live?

  GG GG EE E
  I live in Aberdeen.

- The children reply using only the notes G and E.
- Ideally, every child should have the opportunity to sing back individually. There will always be a few children who are reluctant to sing by themselves but it is worth persevering by giving them the opportunity and not making any fuss if they choose not to sing alone at the particular time of asking.
- Most children will be happy and able to give an answer using two notes. Some children may get the general gap between the notes correct but not the actual pitch – this will come with maturity and practice.

Variation

- Once the children have had a lot of practice with two notes, you could introduce the note la from the solfa staircase which would be sung on the note A.

Cross-curricular links

Language – question and answer techniques, forming a sentence.
Topic work – this activity could be used with any topic being studied, making the questions about information the children have learned through the topic.

Wacky Words

Suitable for

KS1, KS2

Aims

- To allow children to experiment with their voices.
- To give children an opportunity to show emotion when using their voices.
- To give children an opportunity to listen and respond to an auditory stimulus.

Resources

- A list of possible words that the children can experiment with, e.g. happy; surprised; angry; worried; mysterious; nasty; dreamy; snooty; sad; painful; wicked; frightened.

What to do

- Ask a child to choose one of the words and they have to use their voice to illustrate the word.
- The other children in the group have to try and guess what the word is.
- Whoever guesses correctly can be the next person to illustrate a word using their voice.

Variation

- For older children, extend one word to a phrase and they have to use only their voice to illustrate the phrase, e.g. mending a broken tap, greeting someone you haven't seen for a long time, waking up in the morning.

Cross-curricular links

Language – understanding words that convey an emotion, adjectives.
Drama – being able to convey a meaning through sound and action.

One Word at a Time

Suitable for

KS1, KS2

Aims

- To encourage children to sing solo and to still be part of a larger group.
- To develop the children's confidence in singing.

Resources

- A list of songs that everyone in the group will know, e.g.

  'Happy Birthday'
  'Head, Shoulders, Knees and Toes'
  'If You're Happy and You Know It'
  'Ten Green Bottles'
  'Old MacDonald Has a Farm'
  'My Bonnie Lies Over the Ocean'

What to do

- Have the children sitting in a circle and start off by getting the whole group to sing the chosen song together.
- Next, the leader starts off by singing the first word and then asks each child in turn to sing one word around the circle.
- Try to encourage the children to keep in time as the song moves around the circle and hopefully the children will help each other to keep in tune!

Variation

- Start as before with one person but go around the circle in both directions at the same time. The crossover point will be the trickiest part of this activity.

Cross-curricular links

Language – linking words to make sentences, dividing a song/poem into single words.
PSHE – working together for a common goal, confidence building, supporting each other.

The Human Scale

Suitable for

KS1, KS2

Aims

- To develop the children's use of the solfa **scale** (see pp. 7, 8, 9).
- To encourage good listening skills whilst singing.

Resources

- A copy of the solfa staircase with the people on it

What to do

- Practise with the whole class singing up and down the staircase.
- Try asking the whole class to sing some sequences which jump rather than step between notes, e.g.

  doe, me, so, so, me, so, doe, doe
  So, doe, so, me, so, me, so, doe
  Ray, fa, la, fa, la, fa, ray

- Once the children are quite confident with singing any combination of notes from the solfa staircase, assign one note to each child.
- In a class of thirty children there will be a few whose job it is to sing each of the notes from the solfa staircase.
- Using the solfa staircase as 'music', the leader points to the note on the staircase they wish to hear and any child with that note designated to them sings it.
- It is probably best to start with fairly easy, short tunes to increase confidence before moving on to more complicated phrases.

Variation

- The melodies of well-known songs like 'Twinkle, Twinkle, Little Star' could be put into solfa and sung by the Human Scale, e.g.

  Doe, doe, so, so, la, la, so, fa, fa, me, me, ray, ray, doe
  La, la, so, so, fa, fa, me
  La, la, so, so, fa, fa, me
  Doe, doe, so, so, la, la, so, fa, fa, me, me, ray, ray, doe.

Cross-curricular links

Maths – recognising and continuing patterns.
Language – memorising words and thinking them whilst singing something else.

Advanced

'Red Riding Hood'

Suitable for

KS1

Aims

- To encourage the use of singing to enhance storytelling
- To enable the children to identify a character by their song
- To encourage the children to be aware of the ascending/descending/repeated patterns in the songs

Resources

- The leader of this activity needs to have a copy of the songs and be able to sing those songs confidently
- The children could be given a copy of either the words or the words and melody line but the songs can be taught quite easily by rote

What to do

- Go over the story of 'Red Riding Hood' with the class.
- Identify the characters in the story.
- Discuss the different personality traits of the four characters.
- Teach Red Riding Hood's song first of all:

C	D	E	C	D	E	F	E	D	E
Skip	a –	long,	skip	a –	long,	Red	Ri –	ding	Hood.

A	A	A	G	F	E	F	E	D	C
Skip	a –	long,	skip	a –	long,	going	through	the	woods.

- Tell the story and every time Red Riding Hood is mentioned, the children sing her song.

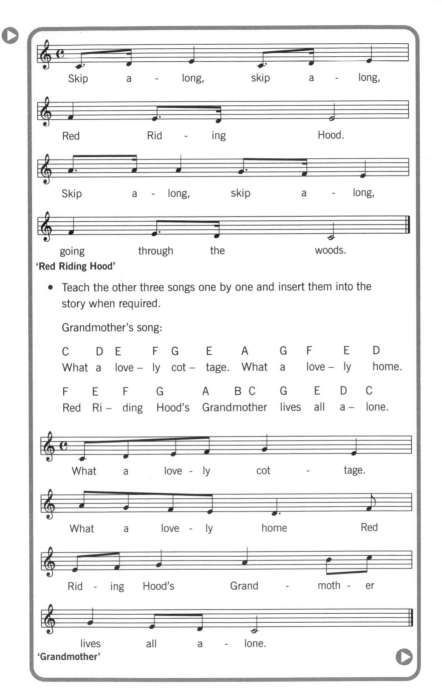

'Red Riding Hood'

- Teach the other three songs one by one and insert them into the story when required.

Grandmother's song:

C	D	E		F	G		E		A		G	F		E		D
What	a	love –	ly	cot –	tage.	What	a		love –	ly		home.

F		E		F		G		A		B	C		G		E	D	C
Red	Ri –	ding	Hood's	Grandmother	lives	all	a –	lone.

'Grandmother'

Wolf's song:

lowC	lowB	lowC	lowC	lowB	lowC	G	G	G	G	lowC
Gree – dy		wolf,	gree – dy		wolf,	what	a	gree – dy		wolf!

Gree - dy wolf.

Gree - dy wolf.

What a gree - dy

wolf.

'Greedy Wolf'

Variations

- Appropriate percussion instruments could be added to accompany each song.
- The class could divide into four groups and each group is responsible for the singing and playing of one song.

Cross-curricular links

Language – storytelling, story writing, analysis of characters in a story.
PSHE – working as part of a team.

'We've Got a House for You'

Suitable for

KS1, KS2

Aims

- To encourage part singing with several parts happening at once.
- To add rhythmic patterns to a song.

Resources

- A copy and/or recording of the song 'We've Got a House for You'
- A CD player
- A selection of untuned percussion instruments, e.g. rhythm sticks, woodblock, tambourine and tambour

What to do

- Let the children hear the song and listen as the various parts are added in.
- There are three singing parts and four rhythmic parts so divide the class first into three for the singing parts.
- Teach one of the very short parts to each of the three groups and let them practise singing their part until they are confident with it.
- Play the recording of the song and add the three vocal parts.
- Next teach the rhythmic parts to the whole group and then let them decide which feature of the house they will be playing.
- When the song is sung through again, each child has responsibility for one singing part and one rhythmic part.

'We've Got a House for You'

de - sign-er   kit - chen

el - e - va - ted   pos - i - tion

child safe   cul - de - sac

pat - i - o   doors

well ap - poin - ted

pan - or - a - mic   view

res - i - den - tial   ar - e - a

Variation

• All the parts can be played rhythmically without any singing taking place.

Cross-curricular links

Language – vocabulary and rhythm of words.
PSHE – confidence building with having responsibility for choosing and maintaining two parts.

Super Scales

Suitable for

KS1, KS2

Aims

- To encourage the children to sing in two parts.
- To develop the children's knowledge of a **major scale**.
- To relate this singing to the solfa scale.

Resources

- A copy of the solfa staircase and people

What to do

- Show the children the solfa staircase and ask them to sing fairly slowly, first up the stairs and then down the stairs starting on the note C.
- They are singing an ascending and descending major scale of C.
- Divide the class into two and ask one half to sing the scale starting on C but when they reach the solfa person called 'me', the other half start at the beginning on 'doe'.
- The children are then singing in **thirds**, e.g. when one group are on E the other group is on C.
- Swap the groups over and repeat this exercise.

Variations

- This activity can be extended by letting the children try to sing in **sixths**.
- This is much harder than thirds but possible with a lot of practice; group 1 would start on 'doe' and group 2 would come in when they reach 'la'.

Cross-curricular links

Maths – recognising patterns and continuing them.

Solfa School Uniform

Suitable for

KS1, KS2

Aims

- To encourage the use of solfa and to develop the use of the solfa staircase.
- To reinforce understanding of the terms **introduction** and coda.
- To sing for enjoyment.

Resources

- A copy of the solfa staircase with people on it
- A copy and/or recording of the 'Uniform Calypso' for each child
- Maracas for accompanying the calypso

What to do

- Sing the song through and personalise it for your own school.
- Ask the children to notice that the piece of music at both the beginning and the end of the song is the same.
- A piece of music played before you start a song is called an introduction and a piece of music at the end of a song is called the coda.
- In this song the introduction and coda are the same music.
- Point out the solfa names for each section of the music:

Doe	so	la		
Fa	la	so		
Doe	so	la		
So	fa	me	ray	doe

- Try singing each section using the solfa names. Join all the sections together and add 'cha, cha, cha' on the maracas after each secion:

Doe	so	la	(cha, cha, cha)
Fa	la	so	(cha, cha, cha)

Doe	so	la	(cha, cha, cha)		
So	fa	me	ray	doe	(cha, cha, cha)

- Now sing the song adding the sung introduction and coda and with maracas playing cha, cha, cha at the appropriate places.
- It is possible to have the maracas during the singing of the verses. In verse 1, there is only room for 'cha, cha' after 'day', 'way' and 'tie'. 'Cha, cha, cha' can be played after 'school'. In verse 2, 'cha, cha, cha' will fit after 'bright', 'right' and 'by' but only 'cha, cha' will fit after 'tie'.

Variations

- Do a hula dance whilst the music for the introduction and coda are being played.
- As well as or instead of singing the solfa names, the notes could be played on tuned percussion. The notes are: D A B, G B A, D A B, A G F$^{\#}$ E D.

Cross-curricular links

Topic work – could fit with a topic about school or clothes.
PE – the hula dance encourages creative movement.

1. When we go to school each day,
2. Are the col - ours bright?

we dress in a spe - cial way. Let's you know just
Red, green, grey that's right. Check the badge and

where we go. We go to Kings - wells school.
check the tie. All of us walk on by.

'Uniform Calypso'

Name That Tune!

Suitable for

KS1, KS2

Aims

- To develop listening skills and concentration.
- To encourage the use of the voice.
- To revise well-known songs.

Resources

- A list of well-known songs e.g.:
  'Happy Birthday'
  'If You're Happy and You Know It'
  'Twinkle, Twinkle, Little Star'
  'The Grand Old Duke of York'
  'The Hokey Cokey'

What to do

- Have the children sitting or standing in a circle and discuss which songs they feel they know very well.
- Ask the children, as a group, to hum the tune of any songs they suggest.
- Start with the leader humming the first two notes of a song and see if the children can guess which song is being hummed.
- Listen to a few suggestions and then hum the first three notes and see if that makes things any clearer.
- Continue adding notes until the children all agree on the song title.
- Once the children are confident with that way of playing the game, ask if any child would like to try being the leader and get them to do the humming.
- It is worth noting that in the list of songs above, the first three titles all start with two repeated notes so singing the first two notes would only eliminate two out of the five songs.
- Obviously, the longer the list of well-known songs, the harder the guessing becomes.

Variations

- Instead of humming the notes, tap out the rhythm of the words either on your hand or with an instrument such as a woodblock or drum.
- To make it much harder, don't have a list of songs. Just choose a song that you know the class are familiar with – this leaves the possibilities wide open and so makes the guessing much harder.

Cross-curricular links

Language – connecting words with rhythm and melody.
PSHE – confidence building.

Body Solfa

Suitable for

KS1, KS2

Aims

- To encourage singing with solfa.
- To aid understanding of notes moving up or down – using body actions.
- To encourage composition with solfa singing.

Resources

- Picture of solfa people on the staircase (see pp. 7, 8 ,9)
- Voices and bodies

What to do

- Go over the solfa names starting with doe at the bottom of the staircase.
- Each solfa person relates to a part of the body so when singing doe at the bottom of the staircase, point to your foot.
- For ray point to your shin and for me point to your knee.
- Experiment using only doe, ray and me and make up little tunes to be echoed whilst pointing to the appropriate part of your body, e.g.

Foot	knee	knee,	knee	shin	foot,	foot	shin
knee	shin	foot	knee
Doe	me	me,	me	ray	doe,	doe	ray
me	ray	doe	me

- Gradually add more people and compose songs using the people covered so far.

  - For fa point to your tummy
  - For so point to your chest
  - For la point to your shoulder
  - For tee point to your nose
  - For doe at the top of the staircase point to the top of your head.

Variation

- Play the game in pairs with one person echoing and pointing whatever tune their partner makes up.

Cross-curricular links

Language – positional words.
PSHE – connecting a musical sound to a position on the body.
       – coordination.

Chapter 2
Playing

Introduction

'Every musical phrase has a purpose. It's like talking. If you talk with a particular purpose, people listen to you, but if you just recite, it's not meaningful.' Itzhak Perlman

The playing activities cover a wide range of abilities and can all be adapted to suit older or younger children. In all the activities, there is an assumption that there will be musical instruments available for the class to use. A modest amount of instruments is essential in order to give the children a meaningful chance to make music. I would hope that any class of 30 children would have enough tuned instruments for two children to share (i.e. 15 instruments) and enough beaters for each child to have two beaters each. In my opinion, you should start as you mean to go on and introduce even the youngest children to the idea of using turnabout beaters whenever they play. It is my experience that very young children are quite capable at trying this playing technique and in fact become proficient fairly quickly.

I feel it is important to give the children every opportunity to learn the correct words and phrases in music and I always tell them the 'adult' way of describing a musical concept, i.e. octave, glissando, ascending, descending, etc. There is a music glossary on p. 285 which gives a simple explanation of all the terms I use in this book. Most children have no difficulty at all in recalling these words and their meanings.

There are several possibilities for music notation and I have used traditional stave notation, solfa notation and simply writing out the letter names of the notes to be played. It is entirely up to the adult using the activities to gauge whether or not their pupils will be able to learn a new or different system. The key is consistency and trying to keep as much of the learning the same as what has gone before. In all the activities there is a mixture of scales, songs, raps, pictorial representation of the music, the use of tuned and untuned percussion instruments.

There are nine advanced activities in this section:

- extend the use of scales and introduces scales which use sharps and flats.
- use wrapping paper as the inspiration for music making.
- introduce simple major chords and gets the children themselves to work out the notes required for each chord.
- move on in the use of chords to composing a round and then performing the round.
- 12-bar blues with an opportunity for children to improvise.

- to have four different parts playing at the same time.
- use a song to encourage singing, rapping and playing the instrumental parts.
- extend the whole idea of a solfa staircase and also reaches into the science of music.
- to introduce some ideas for keyboard skills.

Happy playing!

'Hickory Dickory Dock'

Suitable for

KS1

Aim

- To add sound effects to a nursery rhyme.
- To gain experience in choosing and playing appropriate percussion instruments.

Resources

- The rhyme which the children should be able to recite and should know well
- As wide a selection of percussion instruments as possible

What to do

- Recite the rhyme.
- Start with the first line and decide what instrument could be used for the sound of a clock, e.g. rhythm sticks, claves, woodblock.
- Say the first two-lines: 'Hickory, dickory, dock, the mouse ran up the clock' and then make the sound of the ticking clock for an agreed number of beats.
- At the line 'The mouse ran up the clock', play an ascending **glissando** (slide the beater from the lowest or largest note to the highest or smallest note).
- At the line 'The clock struck one', use a chime bar or glockenspiel to chime one o'clock.
- At the line 'The mouse ran down', play a descending glissando (slide the beater from the top or smallest note to the low or largest note.
- At the last line 'Hickory, dickory, dock', play the ticking sound afterwards to finish the rhyme.

Variation

- Have the ticking sound as a constant during the saying of the rhyme and add in the other sound effects as the rhyme progresses.

Cross·curricular links

Maths – time (o'clocks) and counting.

Language – describing the way the mouse moves, how the clock ticks.

PSHE – working as part of a team.

'Grand Old Duke of York'

Suitable for

KS1

Aims

- To add sound effects to a nursery rhyme.
- To gain experience in choosing and playing appropriate percussion instruments.

Resources

- The rhyme which the children should be able to recite and should know well
- As wide a selection of percussion instruments as possible

What to do

- Recite the rhyme.
- Talk about what happens in the rhyme, e.g.
  - Who is a Duke?
  - How many is ten thousand?
  - What directions did they march in?
  - How do you measure halfway?
- Use the solfa staircase to help with the description of up, down and halfway.
- Say the first line: 'Oh the Grand Old Duke of York' and decide how to do a fitting fanfare for such an important gentleman, e.g. if a class member plays a brass instrument, use that or play a repeated rhythm on a single note on a glockenspiel.
- Say the next line: 'He had ten thousand men' and decide how to represent so many men, e.g. lots of rhythm sticks clicking together for their feet marching around.
- Say the next line: 'He marched them up to the top of the hill and he marched them down again' – decide how to play the marching, e.g. play an ascending **scale** of C – C D E F G A B C – then play a glissando for the descending part (slide the beater from the smallest note to the largest note).

Alternatively, you could play the descending scale of C for the marching down.

- Say the next line: 'And when they were up, they were up' – play the smallest (highest) bar twice.
- Say the next line: 'And when they were down, they were down' – play the largest (lowest) bar twice.
- Say the next line: 'And when they were only halfway up' – play a note in the middle of the instrument but play it **tremolo** (two beaters rapidly turnabout on the same bar).
- Say the last line: 'They were neither up' – play one high note – 'nor down' – play two low notes.

Variation

- Have a soundtrack of a march playing as a background to the whole recital.

Cross-curricular links

Language – describing what is happening in the rhyme.
Maths – positional vocabulary.
Science – small = high sound and large = low sound.

Leap and Jump!

Suitable for

KS1

Aims

- To encourage an understanding of notes that leap rather than step.
- To introduce an octave jump.
- To encourage listening whilst playing and singing.

Resources

- A copy of the song sheet 'Dressed for Fun' for every child
- A tuned percussion instrument for every two children
- Two matching beaters for each instrument

What to do

- Teach the song, adding actions where appropriate.
- Explain that we are going to add some sounds in the spaces between some of the words.
- Sing the song again and let the children notice where the gaps are, i.e. after 'ice', 'nice', 'hat' and 'that'.
- Next do some exploring of the instruments.
- Point out that if you start on any letter and count that note as one, when you reach eight you will come to the same letter.
- Try playing low C then high C, low F then high F, low E then high E, etc.
- In music we call this jump of eight notes an **octave**.
- In the song we need an octave A after the word 'ice' and after the word 'hat'.
- You can play an octave from low to high or from high to low.
- Tell the children that we are going to play from high to low and ask them which size of bar they will need to start on – small bar.
- Sing the song again adding the octave As after 'ice' and 'hat'.
- Next add an octave D after 'nice'.
- Sing the song again with the octaves all played in the correct places.

- At the end of the song, after 'that', we are going to play a jump but it is not as big as an octave.
- The notes we need are A then D.
- Again, the children can decide whether to play A followed by a higher (smaller bar) D or A followed by a lower (bigger bar) D.
- Finally, sing the song and add all the leaps and jumps.

Variations

- Either a separate group of children or the whole class could add appropriate sound effects after the words 'ice', 'nice', 'hat' and 'that'.
- Suggestions for instruments: after 'ice' – sleigh bells, after 'nice' – swannee whistle, after 'hat' – tambourine and after 'that' – woodblock.
- Another variation is to play (not sing) the song and ask the children to play their octaves and jump at the correct place. To do this the children will have to be thinking the words and melody of the song and playing at the appropriate place.

Cross·curricular links

Science – the effects of cold on people and how we can keep warm.
Topic work – could fit with a topic on weather or clothes.

'Dressed for Fun'

Count the Cold

Suitable for

KS1

Aims

- To play descending and stepping notes using **taa** and **tate** rhythms.
- To use a song as the stimulus for a maths lesson.
- To encourage the reading of notes using traditional **stave** notation.

Resources

- A copy of the song sheet 'The Winter Shop' for every child and a recording of the song
- A CD player
- A tuned percussion instrument for every two children
- Two matching beaters for each instrument

What to do

- Listen to the song and then sing it.
- Discuss what would be suitable prices for the items pictured under the song (obviously, the prices used will reflect the level of maths the children are at).
- Look at the notes printed at the top of the song sheet.
- Using the traditional rhyme: '**E**very **G**ood **B**oy **D**eserves **F**ootball', explain that a note on the bottom line is called E, a note on the second line is called G, third line B, fourth line D and fifth line F.
- You know if a note is on a line, because there will be a line through the centre of the note.
- To remember the note names for the spaces you need only the word **F A C E**. The bottom space is called F, second space A, third space C and fourth space E.
- Using these two rhymes, ask the children to work out the note names for the introduction:

  F F E E D C B A G F E D

- The F that is at the beginning of the music is on the top line of the stave so that means it is high F and will be played on a small bar.
- Thereafter, the notes descend in step so they are all next to each other.
- Point out that the first four notes are taa notes and the next eight are tate notes.
- The first four notes will be played at half the speed of the next eight notes.
- Make sure the children use **turnabout beaters** to play the introduction.
- The pairs sharing the tuned percussion instrument can take turnabout playing for each verse.

Variation

- If enough beaters are available for each child to have two beaters, you could ask one child to play the first four notes: F F E E and the other child to play the last eight notes: D C B A G F E D.

Cross-curricular links

Maths – the song is the stimulus for maths work.
Science – large bar = low note, small bar = high note.
The bars get smaller as your notes ascend and larger as your notes descend.
Topic work – would fit with a topic on weather, clothes or shops.

'The Winter Shop'

Explore and Extend

Suitable for

KS1

Aims

- To allow exploration of the different sounds that can be produced using one instrument.
- To develop the children's awareness of different ways to play an instrument.
- To encourage confidence in playing percussion instruments.

Resources

- A wide selection of percussion instruments that can be passed around a circle

What to do

- Have the class sit in a circle and ask the children to suggest a part of the body they can make a sound with.
- Suggestions such as hands, feet, knees, cheeks should come up.
- As each child makes a suggestion, everyone in the circle tries out making the sound, e.g. clap hands, rub hands together, pat knees and pat cheeks.
- Once this area has been explored fully, choose an instrument which can be passed around the circle, e.g. maraca, tambour, guiro.
- Ask each child to play the instrument and then pass it to the next person.
- Each child is free to play the instrument in any way they like.
- This means there is no pressure on any child to come up with a novel way of playing the instrument but should they wish to be adventurous, they can try an unusual way of making a sound on the instrument.
- As the children are trying out ways of playing the instruments, encourage them to describe what they are doing, e.g. 'I'm scraping the guiro', 'I'm shaking the maraca', 'I'm tapping the maraca', 'I'm scraping my fingernail on the tambour.'

Variation

- Once the children have played the instruments many times, pass the instrument and ask for each child to come up with a different way of playing it. When the possibilities are exhausted, give them a different instrument to continue with.

Cross-curricular links

Language – descriptive language, developing knowledge of instrument names.
PE – developing ideas for body movements.

Instrument Squares

Suitable for

KS1, KS2

Aims

- To develop **grid notation**.
- To encourage counting and playing to a beat.
- To develop inventing skills.

Resources

- Some prepared grids:
  Eight squares in a line with the numbers 1–8 above
  Two lots of eight squares, one under the other
  4 × 8 squares labelled with instrument choices
  4 × 8 squares with instrument pictures in the boxes
- CDs for backing
- A selection of percussion instruments

What to do

- Give the children an eight-square grid and ask them to choose an untuned percussion instrument.
- The children choose which squares they want to play in and either write their instrument name in the square or draw a picture of it.
- Once they have practised playing their part correctly, join two then four grids together and play them first individually then gradually add them one at a time until all four are playing at the same time.
- The children will quickly realise that the sounds are better if each instrument plays a different selection of squares with a little overlapping.

Variation

- In groups of four, the children invent their own piece using grid notation. They choose the instrumentation and the squares each instrument plays on. To provide some form for the piece they could invent one grid – called A, do a different grid – called B, then repeat grid A again. This gives a structure called **Ternary form** – ABA, **Binary form** would be AB or AABB.

Cross-curricular links

Maths – patterns, counting, binary and ternary forms.
PSHE – working together to create a piece.

Shake that Skeleton

Suitable for

KS1, KS2

Aims

- To consolidate information about bones in the body.
- To encourage invention in the playing of classroom instruments.
- To produce a piece of music about the skeleton.

Resources

- A CD of the song 'Dry Bones'
- A wide selection of tuned and untuned percussion instruments
- A picture of a skeleton with the bones labelled (available to download from the website)

What to do

- Play the song 'Dry Bones' and perhaps make up a little dance to go along with it which would involve the children in moving each bone as it is mentioned.
- Look at the picture of the skeleton and explain that we are going to use a two-line rhyme for each bone and then choose appropriate percussion instruments to accompany the rhyme.
- Start with the foot and chant the rhyme:

  Go for a walk, stamp your feet
  Down the street to the funky beat

- Decide which instrument (s) would best suit this rhyme and its action and add the sound to the saying of the rhyme.
- Continue to do this all the way up the skeleton until you have a whole piece of skeleton music.
- The rhymes for each bone are as follows but it would be just as good to make up your own rhymes.

  ANKLES: Ankles can dance, help you twirl
  　　　Twist and turn, do a jazzy swirl.

SHIN: Swing your shin, don't fall back
  Play football, do a sliding attack.
KNEES: Bend your knees, exercise
  If you do, you'll be healthy and wise.
THIGHS: Slap your thighs, side to side
  Eat those pies and you'll turn out wide.
HIPS: Wiggle your hips, do a dance
  Wiggle your hips if you get a chance.
SHOULDERS: Shrug your shoulders up and down
  Side to side when you swagger to town.
BACK: Bend your back, stand up straight
  Take a bow 'cos you look great.
HEAD: At the top, there's your head
  Nod up and down; yes that's what I said.

- Suggested instruments for each bone would be:
    Feet – rhythm sticks or claves
    Ankles – cabasa
    Shin – pinging your finger on a tambour
    Knees – chatterbox/vibraslap
    Thighs – whip
    Hips – two bars on a xylophone that are next to each other, played rapidly one after the other
    Back – on a glockenspiel, playing low C followed by high C followed by low C
    Shoulders – on a xylophone, sliding a beater up and down between about five notes
    Head – woodblock playing a 'nodding' beat.

- These are simply suggestions; the children will have a lot more ideas!

Variations

- Leave out the rhymes and just choose a sound for each bone.
- Record your skeleton music using the skeleton picture as a score and the conductor points to the appropriate bone and that group then plays.
- Listen to the recording and try to identify which bone is being played.

Cross-curricular links

Science – the human body and how bones work.

Language – finding appropriate adjectives for the action that each bone makes.

PE – trying out different ways of moving for each part of the skeleton, coordination.

Up and Down and Turnabout

Suitable for

KS1, KS2

Aims

- To play an ascending and descending one-octave scale of C major.
- To familiarise pupils with the layout of standard classroom percussion instruments – **diatonic** (without sharps or flats) and **chromatic** (with sharps and flats).
- To play a tuned percussion instrument using two beaters.

Resources

- A tuned percussion instrument for every two pupils in the class (a glockenspiel has metal bars and a xylophone has wooden bars)
- Two matching beaters for each instrument

What to do

- Explain to the class that a scale is a set of notes which step up or step down.
- A set of eight notes is called an octave and the scale we are going to play starts on the note C.
- Low C is the large bar marked C on the glockenspiel or xylophone. (The same note on a piano or keyboard is called middle C as it is found in exactly the middle of the keyboard.)
- Ask the class to play the low C using turnabout beaters. (Hold the beaters with the thumb pressing on the stick and the fingers curled around the stick), e.g.

  C   C   C
  Right beater, left beater, right beater

- Practise with the teacher playing first then an echo by the class.
- The teacher plays again to give time for the partners to pass the beaters and echo the second time.
- Continue in this manner playing C, D, E, F, G, A, B, C.

- The music will sound thus:

  Teacher plays C, C, C, rest   Pupils play C, C, C, rest (repeat this for partner echoes)
  Teacher plays D, D, D, rest   Pupils play D, D, D, rest (repeat this for partner echoes)
  Teacher plays E, E, E, rest   Pupils play E, E, E, rest (repeat this for partner echoes)
  Teacher plays F, F, F, rest   Pupils play F, F, F, rest (repeat this for partner echoes)
  Teacher plays G, G, G, rest   Pupils play G, G, G, rest (repeat this for partner echoes)
  Teacher plays A, A, A, rest   Pupils play A, A, A, rest (repeat this for partner echoes)
  Teacher plays B, B, B, rest   Pupils play B, B, B, rest (repeat this for partner echoes)
  Teacher plays C, C, C, rest   Pupils play C, C, C, rest (repeat this for partner echoes)

- Once that has been achieved, the pupils can try playing the ascending scale with single notes using turnabout beaters, e.g.

  C   D   E   F   G
  Right beater, left beater, right beater, left beater, right beater,

  A   B   C
  left beater, right beater, left beater

- Next repeat the whole procedure but start on high C and step downwards, e.g.

  C   B   A   G   F   E   D   C

Variation

- Play the ascending or descending notes to a pattern of words, e.g.

  C   C   C C C   D D   D D D
  Stepping up a scale, beaters turnabout,
  E   E E E E   E   F   F   F   F F
  Playing ascending notes, now you'll hear us shout,

```
G G  G   G G A    A A    A A
```
In the scale of C, there's no sharps or flats,
```
B   B    B     B  B  C   C   C   C C
```
Now we've reached the top, what d'you think of that!
```
C   C   C C  C   B   B   B   B B
```
Starting at the top, stepping slowly down,
```
A   A A A   A    G    G   G G   G
```
Now descending notes, that's what we have found,
```
F   F   F  F  F    E E E E    E
```
Counting out the notes, in an octave – eight,
```
D   D   D     D  D   C   C  C   C   C
```
Now we've reached the end, don't you think we're great!

Cross·curricular links

Make up a rhyme pertinent to the topic being studied, e.g.
History – Vikings
(Viking women's household chores (C). Here's a list can you think of more (D)?
Spin the thread, weave cloth (E). Fetch water; make some broth (F).
Sweep the floor, dry some fish (G). Feed the baby from a homemade dish (A).
Gather eggs, bake bread (B). Keep all these chores stored in your head (C).)
History – Romans
(Get up early when in Rome (C). Use a lantern when leaving home (D).
Boys wear loincloth, tunic too (E). If it's cold, short cloak will do (F).
Men wear a toga, women a shawl (G). Slaves aren't allowed a toga at all (A).
Children wear a bulla, necklace charm (B). Just to keep them safe from harm (C).)
Maths – counting, stepping, sequencing.
PSHE – coordination – using beaters turn about and with the correct hold.

Cabbage Patch Countdown

Suitable for

KS1, KS2

Aims

- To become familiar with traditional **treble clef** stave notation.
- To be able to find a note on a glockenspiel or xylophone using stave notation.

Resources

- A tuned percussion instrument for every two pupils in the class
- Two matching beaters for each instrument
- A board for writing up the five lines and four spaces of the stave
- Some manuscript paper

What to do

- Explain to the class that the musical alphabet uses only seven letters:

  A   B   C   D   E   F   G

- As a writing exercise, ask the children to make up as many words as they can from these seven letters, e.g.: age, deaf, ace, bag, cabbage, face, bad, bead, badge.
- Having made up the words, the children then write the corresponding notes on the stave (or the teacher could do this).
- In pairs, the children compete with each other to try and play the words as quickly as possible.
- In order to do this, each child has to decipher the code, i.e. read the musical notes and transfer that into playing the associated tune.
- The listening and timing partner also has to work out the notes in order to check that their partner is giving them the correct answer.

Variation

- Give a set amount of time for each word i.e. 20 seconds for a three-letter word, 30 seconds for a four-letter word, one minute for a seven-letter word and ask the children to beat the clock.

Cross-curricular links

Language – linking with letter recognition, spelling and vocabulary.
Maths – timing the activity, using a stopwatch.
Problem solving – decoding and working out either the solution or checking the answer is correct.
PSHE – team working, partner consideration, using beaters turn about and with the correct hold.

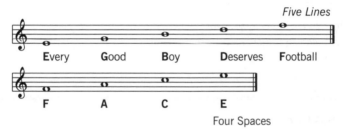

Five Lines

Every   Good   Boy   Deserves   Football

F   A   C   E

Four Spaces

Stave Notation

Bubble Bounce

Suitable for

KS1, KS2

Aims

- For children to become confident in playing tuned percussion instruments.
- To introduce **tremolo** playing – using two beaters alternately but very quickly on one bar to create a continuous trembling sound.
- The best tremolo playing requires very gentle but rapid alternating beaters.
- To reinforce the concept of descending notes.

Resources

- A tuned percussion instrument for every two pupils in the class
- Two matching beaters for each instrument
- Bubble-blowing equipment

`What to do

- Ask the children to start on the highest notes of their instrument (smallest bars) and practise playing tremolo – alternate beaters gently and rapidly on one bar.
- The 'bubble blower' (could be an adult or a child) then blows some bubbles and asks the children to watch the bubbles.
- Each child should then choose one bubble to watch and follow it until it reaches the ground and bursts.
- Next the child watches the bubble and plays tremolo notes to follow the direction the bubble moves in, e.g.:

```
    O
  O   O
  O   O
      O
      O
        O
```

- The note playing needs to reflect the gentle nature of the bubbles, i.e., no walloping of the bars!
- Finally, the child follows the bubble, playing tremolo notes and when it bursts, they hit the bar they have reached once.

Variations

- The pair of children sharing an instrument could sit on opposite sides of it and 'play' their own bubbles simultaneously – four beaters per instrument would be needed for this.
- To produce a piece of bubble music, you could dictate whether xylophone (wooden bars) or glockenspiel (metal bars) should be played at certain points.

Cross-curricular links

Science – what direction do the bubbles go in? Is it always the same – predictable? Does the tremolo playing affect the bubbles?
PSHE – working as a team, partner consideration, using turnabout beaters and with the correct hold.

'Ready to Go!'

Suitable for

KS1, KS2

Aims

- To use the techniques of glissando and octaves in a song.
- To use an instrument called a vibraslap/chatterbox.
- To play an instrumental part whilst keeping to a beat already established.

Resources

- A recording of the song 'Ready to Go'
- A tuned percussion instrument for every two children
- Two matching beaters for each instrument
- A copy of the song sheet 'Ready to Go' for each child (or pair of children)
- A vibraslap or chatterbox

What to do

- Let the children hear a recording of the song.
- At the end of the song there are sound effects for running, jumping and hopping.
- Ask the children to describe the sounds they can hear.
- Explain that the sound used for the running is called a glissando and is played by sliding the beater from one end of the instrument to the other (from the biggest bar to the smallest bar for an ascending glissando or from the smallest bar to the biggest bar for a descending glissando).
- Ask the children to experiment with playing a glissando and then decide if they want to have ascending or descending glissandi or a mixture of both.
- Next explain about the octaves (see p. 82).
- An **octave** is a jump of eight notes and is always from one of the same name as the one being landed on, e.g., from low F to high F in this song.

- Ask the children to practise playing their octaves and then try to join the glissando part with the octaves.
- You could have three groups each playing one part.
- Lastly, show the chatterbox and explain how it is played. The hand bounces off the ball to allow the vibration to travel around the metal and make the rattle shake.
- Sing the song and add the sound effects at the end.

Variation

- Think up more races to make sound effects for, e.g. javelin (flying through the air and landing in the grass), sack race (shuffling along sound), skipping race (a skipping rhythm played on the tuned percussion).

Cross-curricular links

Language – a musical representation of various words.
PE – a musical representation of various movements.
Science – how vibrations work, along with explanations of ascending and descending sounds.

'Ready to Go!'

'Pass the Beaters'

Suitable for

KS1, KS2

Aims

- To increase confidence in playing tuned percussion instruments.
- To encourage playing with alternate beaters.
- To develop listening skills.

Resources

- Room for a large circle of children
- A knowledge of the song 'Pass the Beaters'
- A tuned percussion instrument such as a glockenspiel or xylophone
- Two matching beaters

What to do

- Sit the children in a circle with the tuned percussion instrument in the middle.
- Teach the children the song called 'Pass the Beaters':

  Pass the beaters round this way
  If they stop here then I'll play.

- Give one of the children in the circle a pair of beaters to hold in each hand and, as the song is sung, the beaters are passed from child to child.
- Both beaters are passed simultaneously taking care to continue holding them as if ready to play, i.e., with the thumb of each hand pressing on the stick of the beater and all the fingers curled around the beater.
- When the song is sung, whoever has the beaters goes to the instrument in the middle of the circle.
- The leader of this activity has left only a small number of bars on the instrument.

- Depending on the age and ability level of the children, it would be wise to start with only three bars and gradually build up the bars as the children's confidence grows.
- The child with the beater plays a melody using the bars available.
- If there are the notes C D and E to choose from they could play C C C E C.
- The other children in the circle volunteer to try and reproduce the tune that has been played.
- Whoever is successful starts the game off again.

Variations

- When the first child makes up their tune, they say/sing the notes they are playing making it much easier for someone else to reproduce their tune.
- When the first child makes up their tune, they say/sing the notes they are playing and everyone else in the circle has to sing the tune they have played. The beaters then continue round the circle.

Cross-curricular links

PE – practise at moving alternate hands.
PSHE – confidence building, being part of a team, listening to others.
Writing – letter recognition (for younger children).

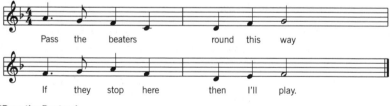

'Pass the Beaters'

Investigate the Instruments

Suitable for

KS1, KS2

Aims

- To increase knowledge of the names of percussion instruments.
- To increase confidence in identifying the sound of percussion instruments.
- To develop listening skills.

Resources

- A wide selection of both tuned and untuned percussion instruments
- Two matching beaters for any tuned percussion instruments

What to do

- The class sit in a circle.
- Give every second child an untuned percussion instrument.
- Give the children in the spaces in between a tuned percussion instrument, preferably a mixture of xylophones, glockenspiels and chime bars.
- The leader walks a blindfolded child around the outside of the circle whilst everyone plays their instrument reasonably quietly.
- After completing the tour, the leader names an instrument and the blindfolded child has to walk around the circle until they hear the sound of that instrument.
- The blindfolded child taps the player on the shoulder and if correct, everyone else stops playing and you hear only the correct instrument.
- If the choice is wrong, the circle keeps playing and the blindfolded child has another chance to find the instrument.
- Once the correct instrument has been found, that player becomes the blindfolded person and the game continues.

Variation

- There is a backing track of instrumental music that everyone is playing along with, making it harder for the blindfolded person to locate the instrument.
- Everyone plays a predetermined rhythm so the person guessing is listening to the same rhythm pattern from everybody. This might make it easier or harder for the person guessing!

Cross-curricular links

Language – really develops listening skills and encourages the learning of the names of the instruments.

PSHE – develops trust in the person leading the blindfolded person and in the group situation. Builds team spirit as everyone has to listen in order to play the game correctly.

Sorting Spot

Suitable for

KS1, KS2

Aims

- To develop the children's awareness that sounds are made in different ways, using different materials.
- To encourage children to explore the different ways to make a sound on an instrument.

Resources

- A wide range of percussion instruments which can be sorted into different groups:

  Skin instruments – drum, tambour, tambourine

  Metal instruments – sleigh bells, Indian bells, cymbals, triangle, cowbell, chime bar

  Shaking instruments – maracas, cabasa

  Scraping instruments – guiro, wooden agogo

  Wooden instruments – woodblock, rhythm sticks, claves, xylophone
- A rug or blanket for the spot in which to do the sorting
- A folded card with the name of each group for sorting the instruments

What to do

- Ask the children to sit in a circle around the spot with all the instruments on it.
- Ask an individual to choose one instrument and describe it to the rest of the group then make a sound on it. The description may go something like this: 'I am holding an instrument made of wood with silver bells around it and a skin top. I am going to tap it.'
- The rest of the group then have to name the instrument and decide which group of instruments it goes into: skin, metal, shaking, scraping or wooden.

- It is worth noting that some instruments will fit into more than one category, e.g., a wooden agogo fits into the wooden group and the scraping group.
- It is also worth pointing out to the children that it is how the sound is made on the instrument that decides which group it goes into and not what it is made of.
- Once the instrument is placed into a group then another child continues with a different instrument until all the instruments have been placed.

Variation

- Once the instruments have been categorised, the class could take a category each and make up their own skin, metal, shaking, scraping and wooden music.

Cross-curricular links

Maths – grouping the instruments into sets.
Language – vocabulary development, listening, auditory discrimination.
Science – observing and recording experiments, investigating similarities and differences.

Stretch a Sound

Suitable for

KS1, KS2

Aims

- To develop the children's imagination in how to produce sounds.
- To encourage children to think 'out of the box' with regard to sounds.
- To enable children to have a lot more options for producing sounds.

Resources

- Several sheets of A4 size paper
- Several elastic bands of different sizes and thicknesses
- Several pieces of cardboard of different thicknesses

What to do

- Ask the children to think of as many different sounds as they can which can be produced using only a sheet of paper, e.g., pinging the paper with a thumb and finger; scrunching it up; ripping it; rubbing your hand over the paper; flapping it; making a shaker by ripping strips which then shake to make a rattling sound; holding the paper firmly at either end and making a cracking sound, etc.
- Either do the same with the whole class for the elastic bands and the cardboard or divide the class into three groups and have a competition to see which group comes up with the most possibilities for sound production.

Variation

- Ask the children to come up with other possibilities for producing sounds, e.g., a tin can; a plastic yoghurt pot; a handful of uncooked rice, etc.

Cross·curricular links

Maths – problem solving.

Language – using words to describe what you are doing to produce the sound.

Craft and design – making something out of 'nothing', being creative in your thinking to produce a sound-maker.

Arpeggio Fanfares

Suitable for

KS1, KS2

Aims

- To develop the children's knowledge of solfa through the use of the **arpeggio**.
- To encourage the children to experiment with notes to produce a **fanfare**.
- To increase the children's confidence in playing tuned percussion instruments.

Resources

- A copy of the solfa staircase (see pp. 8–9) with only red doe, me, so and purple doe in place on the staircase
- A tuned percussion instrument for every two children in the class
- Two matching beaters for each instrument

What to do

- Explain that a fanfare is a piece of music which is used to announce the arrival of someone important.
- Ask the children to sing the notes on the solfa staircase – doe, me, so, doe.
- Sing them from the bottom note to the top note and then back down again.
- Explain that this series of short jumps is called an arpeggio and is a good set of notes to use for making a fanfare.
- Tell the children that if doe is C then the other notes in the arpeggio are E, G and high C.
- Ask the children to experiment with these four notes and compose a short fanfare using them, e.g., C E C E G, high C, high C.
- Once the children are confident at playing this fanfare tell them we are going to move doe and make doe G which means the other notes in the arpeggio are now G B D and high G.

- Ask the children to practise playing this and to try playing the fanfare they composed on these notes, e.g., G B G B D, high G, high G.
- In order to extend their fanfares, ask the children to play version 1 then version 2 then version 1 again.
- If there are two children sharing an instrument, they could play one version each.

Variation

- The children could decide where they want doe to be and practise playing lots of different arpeggios, e.g., D F A, high D or F A C, high F.

Cross-curricular links

Maths – recognising patterns and being able to continue them.
Language – introduction of new words, e.g., fanfare and arpeggio.
PSHE – working together for a common aim, confidence building.

A Weather Picture

Suitable for

KS1, KS2

Aims

- To develop the children's abilities to improvise and produce their own sound picture.
- To allow the children the opportunity to explore the classroom instruments.
- To encourage the children to produce a **graphic score** of their improvisations.

Resources

- A selection of tuned and untuned percussion instruments
- A copy of the ideas list for 'Weather Music' – ideally one for each child (see following page)

What to do

- Let the children have a look at the 'Weather Music' sheet and try out the suggestions as far as instrumentation is concerned.
- Divide the class into groups of five or six children and ask them to be in charge of one weather type.
- Get each group to start off by trying out the suggestions on the sheet, then progressing to adding their own ideas and making an improvisation lasting approximately one minute.
- Once all the groups have decided how they are going to produce their music, they listen to each other and give advice about how the sound could be improved.
- Finally, each group produces a graphic score showing how their music is produced by making images to accompany the music; i.e., a picture of the sun to represent 'sunshine' – the idea being that some other children could come along and read their score to produce similar music.

Variations

- The class could use their individual improvisations to make a much larger piece perhaps a 'Weather Forecast' or a tale of a 'Day Out with Weather Difficulties'.
- The graphic scores could be pinned up in the order they are required for the story and then each group could play at the appropriate time.

Cross-curricular links

Art – producing a visual representation of the music the children have made up.
Language – discussing the appropriate ways of conveying musically the different types of weather and using many different words for all the weather types.
PSHE – working as a team.
Topic work – would fit with a topic on weather.

Weather Music

Sunshine: continuous tremolo on triangle
tremolo notes on glockenspiel
suspended cymbal gently tapped continuously
Rain: fingertips tapping gently on a tambour
gently shaken maracas
high glockenspiel notes played slowly and quietly
– for heavier rain – played more rapidly
Wind: recorder tops blown softly
voices 'ooh' moving up and down
glissando on a glockenspiel
Thunder: very low notes on the piano played with the sustain pedal held down
bass drum roll
Lightning: sharp crash of cymbals

Rainbow: build-up of seven sounds, each one
playing 'on top of' the previous one
Red – drum roll with fingers
Orange – suspended cymbals roll
Yellow – Indian bells tinkling
Green – maraca shaken
Blue – tambourine shaken
Indigo – triangle played tremolo
Violet – handled castanet shaken

'Tell Me Another One'

Suitable for

KS1, KS2

Aims

- To develop the children's ability to read standard **stave** notation.
- To encourage the children to make up their own sentences using musical notation.

Resources

- Tuned percussion instruments and two matching beaters for playing them
- A copy of the lines and spaces of stave notation (see p. 99)
- A copy of the 'Tell Me Another One' sheet
- Some manuscript paper

What to do

- Show the children some of the sample sentences and ask them to use their knowledge of stave notation to work out what the missing words are.
- Once they have written in the letter names ask them to play the musical part of the sentence.
- Have a partner say the sentence and let them pause as the word to be played is played.
- Ask the children to make up their own sentences.
- It is probably a good idea to ask the children to make up a possible words list first which they can refer to when they are writing their sentences.
- Either use manuscript paper or get the children to draw their own staves for writing the words to be played.
- They can then perform their own sentences to each other.

Variations

- Write a whole story using this system.
- Join all the sentences the children have used to make one long story.

Cross·curricular links

Language – formation of sentences, story writing.
Drama – presentation skills, confidence building.

'Tell Me Another One'

'Have You Seen the Leaves?'

Suitable for

KS1, KS2

Aims

- To encourage some creativity using a song as a stimulus.
- To allow the children freedom to experiment with sounds.

Resources

- A copy and/or recording of the song 'Have You Seen the Leaves'
- A CD player
- A selection of tuned and untuned percussion instruments

What to do

- Let the children listen to the song then discuss the words contained in it.
- Divide the song into five sections:

  Have you seen the leaves falling from the trees?
  Have you felt the weather getting colder?
  Nights are getting darker.
  Autumn time is here.
  Did you know the year is getting older?

- Divide the class into five groups and ask each group to be responsible for one of the phrases.
- They must find instruments and sounds that will accurately convey the words in their group's phrase.
- All listen to each group's offerings and give constructive advice on how they could improve their composition.
- Once every group has played and refined their part, join all the parts together to form a whole piece.

Variations

- Have the children sing a phrase and then play their composition.
- Have the children sing the whole song and then play the whole composition.

Cross-curricular links

Language – discussing the descriptive nature of the song words.
PSHE – working as part of a group, sharing and presenting work.
Science – trying out different ways to produce the required sound.

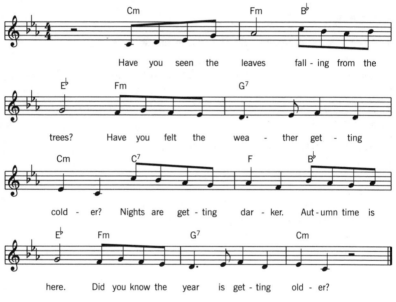

'Have You Seen the Leaves?'

Play Pentatonic

Suitable for

KS1, KS2

Aims

* To introduce the children to the **pentatonic scale**.
* To link the pentatonic scale with the solfa staircase.
* To encourage the children to improvise using the **pentatonic scale**.

Resources

* A tuned percussion instrument for every two children
* A pair of matching beaters for every instrument
* A copy of the solfa staircase with the people doe, ray, me, so and la in place on the staircase

What to do

* Ask the children to play the C scale which uses the notes C D E F G A B C (see p. 95).
* Next, look at the solfa staircase and point out which people have been removed – fa and tee, the fourth and seventh steps.
* Ask the children to work out which notes they need to miss out from their scale – F and B.
* Now ask the children to play their new scale which is called a pentatonic scale because it uses five notes C D E G A.
* Using the phrase 'pentatonic playing' ask the children to compose a phrase using only the notes from the pentatonic scale, e.g., G G A A E E.
* Once every child has had an opportunity to play their composition, ask four children to play their piece one after the other to make a longer phrase.
* Using this method, the class can produce a reasonably long piece.

Variation

- Extend this activity by deciding on a poem or series of phrases (perhaps topic related) that the children could add a melody to using the pentatonic scale.

Cross-curricular links

Language – phrasing, poetry.

Maths – patterns in an **eight-note scale** and a pentatonic scale.

PSHE – confidence building in producing your own composition.

Drastic Droning

Suitable for

KS1, KS2

Aims

- To introduce the children to a **drone** – an **interval** of a fifth.
- To encourage the children to play an **accompaniment** using drones.

Resources

- A tuned percussion instrument for every two children in the class
- A pair of matching beaters for every instrument

What to do

- Ask the children to put one of their beaters on a bar marked C and the other on a bar marked G.
- Play both of these notes at the same time and they have played a drone – the sound bagpipes make when the bag is pressed to allow air to move through the pipes.
- A drone is an interval called a fifth, i.e., counting C as one, G is five notes above C.
- Ask the children to find other drones by choosing a lower note, e.g., F and counting five notes above it – C.
- Once they have experimented with various drones ask the children to try accompanying 'What Shall We Do With the Drunken Sailor?' using drones:

  A   A
  D   D
  What shall we do with the drunken sailor?
  G   G
  C   C
  What shall we do with the drunken sailor?

```
A                        A
D                        D
What shall we do with the drunken sailor?
G        A
C        D
Early in the morning.
```

Variation

- Using their compositions from Play Pentatonic, p. 121, the children could use the drones

```
C   A
G   E
```

to accompany their melodies.

Cross-curricular links

Geography – drones and bagpipes leading to an investigation of Scottish music.
Maths – working out fifths.
Language – new words such as accompaniment, interval, and drone.

Think Sharp

Suitable for

KS1, KS2

Aims

- To play an ascending and descending one octave scale in several different **keys**.
- To familiarise pupils with the layout of standard classroom tuned percussion instruments – particularly the **sharp** (#) bars.
- To play a tuned percussion instrument using two beaters.

Resources

- A tuned percussion instrument for every two pupils in the class
- Two matching beaters for each instrument

What to do

- Remind the children of 'Up and Down and Turnabout' (see p. 95), when they learned how to play a scale starting on C – revise this.
- Try saying the think rhyme then play the scale using it:

  Think when you're in bed – C
  Think inside your head – D
  Think about your day – E
  Think how you will play – F
  Think how you will act – G
  Think – 'cause it's a fact – A
  Thinking helps you see – B
  The best that you can be – C

- Explain that we are now going to start on a different note, i.e., G and that means we now have an F sharp (#) to play.
- The scale is therefore G A B C D E F# G.
- Practise ascending then descending.
- Now try the scale starting on D, which has two sharps:

  D E F# G A B C# D

- For Key Stage 1, it might be best to do only the scale of C and the scale of G and add any others gradually much later.
- If the children are confident with C, G and D scales, you can then add the scale of A which has three sharps: F#, C# and G#.

  A B C# D E F# G# A

- For the scale of E you need four sharps: F# C# G# and D#:

  E F# G# A B C# D# E

- It is possible to go as far as seven sharps, but managing up to four is pretty impressive and you are unlikely to come across music with more than four sharps.

N.B. the sharps always appear in the same order, F# first, then C# then G#, then D#, then A#, then E#, then B#.

Variations

- A simpler rhyme for KS1 could be:

  Can you play (C), day by day (D)
  Everyone (E) having fun? (F)
  Good for you (G), all you do (A)
  Be the best (B), catch the zest! (C)

- In groups of two, ask each other to play different scales, e.g., in the scale that needs two sharps, the partner must remember the starting note and the sharps required. The questioner could also decide whether the scale requested has to be played ascending or descending.

Cross-curricular links

PSHE – positive message for living in the 'Think' rhymes.
Maths – patterns in music/numbers of notes, counting, stepping, sequencing.

Advanced

Wrap Up that Inspiration

Suitable for

KS1, KS2

Aims

- To develop playing skills.
- To encourage composition skills.
- To develop imagination.

Resources

- A variety of patterned wrapping paper, e.g., animals; 'Happy Birthday' written in various sizes with flower patterns; new baby with duck, teddy, rattle, hearts, stars, coochy coo and little one written on it; balloons – green with big spots, long red stripy, green with little spots, pink star-shaped, blue with big spots, long blue with small stars, yellow with big spots, yellow with small spots

What to do

- Select a pattern of wrapping paper and list everything it contains visually (as above).
- Decide how to represent each picture using percussion instruments and/or voices.
- Decide if you want a constant tune, e.g., with the new baby paper you could play or sing a lullaby and add the sounds of all the other pictures on the paper.
- With the Happy Birthday paper you could play snippets of the Happy Birthday tune – loud for big writing and quiet for small writing – and have flowery music interspersed.
- The balloons paper gives huge scope for deciding if small and large = quiet and loud or high and low. Each different balloon pattern could represent a different instrument – the wrapping paper could be the 'music'.

Variations

- Make up a story about the wrapping paper, e.g., animals – their sounds and what they are doing.
- New baby – a story of baby's arrival into a family.

Cross-curricular links

Maths – patterns, sequences, shapes, sizes.
Language – descriptive words, story telling/writing.
Science – big = low sound, small = high sound.

1, 3, 5 and sometimes 7

Suitable for

KS1, KS2

Aims

- To explain the construction of basic **chords** C, F and G7.
- To give children the opportunity to construct and perform simple chord sequences.

Resources

- Tuned percussion instruments, ideally one for every two children in the class
- Two matching beaters for each instrument

> **The best instruments are chime bars and glockenspiels, but xylophones would be fine as well.**

What to do

- Explain that we are going to learn what a chord consists of (two or more notes played together) and how to construct three different chords.
- Basically, the letter name of the chord is the keynote or first note of that chord so in the chord of C, number 1 is C.
- Ask the children to look on their tuned percussion instrument and try to find the largest C bar they can.
- Call that bar number 1 and then work out what numbers 3 and 5 are (E and G).
- Once numbers 1, 3 and 5 have been found, you have the notes for the chord of C.
- Practise playing all three notes at the same time.
- Now do the same with the chord of F and you end up with the notes F, A and C.

- For the chord of G7, the only difference is that you need the seventh note as well. The notes you end up with are G, B, D and F.
- Practise playing all three chords, there are two ways of doing this:
  - Have a group of children for each chord and get them to use their two beaters to play two out of the three notes in their chord.
  - Alternatively, ask the children to choose two notes from each chord and then play their two chosen notes when each chord is played. This is much harder, as the children need to remember what they have chosen from each chord.
- Ask the children to experiment with different chord sequences. It is likely that they will realise eventually that it's better to start and finish with the chord C. Some possibilities are:

C - - -, C - - -, F - - -, F - - -, G7 - - -, G7 - - -, C - - -, C - - -
C - - -, F - - -, G7 - - -, C - - -, G7 - - -, G7 - - -, C - - -, C - - -
C - - -, C - - -, F - - -, F - - -, C - - -, G7 - - -, C - - -, C - - -

It is worth pointing out that the note C is common to chord C (CEG) and chord F (FAC).

Variations

- Using the notes from each chord, it is possible to compose a melody to be played with the chord sequence.
- In chord sequence 1, a simple melody would be:

E - - -, G - - -, F - - -, A - - -, G - - -, F - - -, E - - -, C - - -

Cross-curricular links

PSHE – 'ownership' of their composition, working as part of a team.
Maths – counting and patterns.

Playing a Round

Suitable for

KS1, KS2

Aims

- To encourage the children to experiment with composition using classroom instruments.
- To develop the children's knowledge of chords and how to compose a melody from the notes in a chord.
- To try playing a round that they have composed.

Resources

- A copy of the 'Writing a Round' sheet for each child to write on
- A tuned instrument for every two children in the class
- Two matching beaters for each instrument

What to do

- Show the children the 'Writing a Round' sheet and explain that the three letters in each box are the notes of a chord and they are allowed to choose only one of these notes in order to compose their melody.
- Explain that the **time signature** indicates four beats to each bar and therefore each note is played for four counts.
- The first and last notes of the melody have been set for the children and it is worth pointing out that the chord sequence stays the same for each line of the melody.
- Discuss with the children the fact that it is better for the overall sound to try and have a mixture of repeated notes and stepping notes.
- Explain that they may want to repeat one of the lines of their melody.
- As a class, look at the first line and work out what some of the possibilities are for making up a melody:

  E D C E, E G E G, E D E E, E B E C, etc.

- Ask individuals to play some of the possibilities in order for the children to understand that they will need to try things out before they decide on the melody they want to write down.
- Ask the children to experiment and write one line at a time then try playing it to their partner.
- Once the whole melody has been written, get each child to perform their tune to the rest of the class.
- Make sure a steady beat is kept, perhaps played on a woodblock or drum.
- Finally, take two children and ask one to start their tune and the second child joins in with their tune when the first child reaches line 2.
- Because the chord sequences are the same in each line, the two melodies will fit together when played as a round.

Variations

- Because the notes are all **semibreves** (four-beat notes), the children could play their melodies using a tremolo technique (playing alternate beaters rapidly to make a continuous sound).
- Once the children are very confident at playing their own melodies, you can have a round for four individuals.
- If this is successful, you could have the whole class divided into four groups and all come in to play a round together.

Cross-curricular links

Maths – recognising patterns, strategies for problem solving.
PSHE – working as part of a team, confidence building.

1.

$\frac{4}{4}$	C E G	G B D	C E G	C E G
	E			

2.

C E G	G B D	C E G	C E G

3.

C E G	G B D	C E G	C E G

4.

C E G	G B D	C E G	C E G
			C

Writing a Round

12-Bar Blues

Suitable for

KS1, KS2

Aims

- To develop the use of the chords C, F and G7.
- To give the children the opportunity to improvise using a simple **blues scale**.

Resources

- Tuned percussion instruments, ideally one for every two children in the class.
- Two matching beaters for each instrument. The best instruments are chime bars and glockenspiels but xylophones would be fine as well.

> The note B flat is required and on some instruments it may be necessary to swap the B bar for the B flat bar.

What to do

- Revise the work done in 1, 3, 5 and sometimes 7 (see p. 130).
- Have written on the board, the chord sequence for a 12-bar blues:

```
C - - -    C - - -    C - - -    C - - -
F - - -    F - - -    C - - -    C - - -
G7 - - -   F - - -    C - - -    C - - -
```

- Ask the children to try and play it through choosing two notes from each chord for every child.
- Next tell the children that they are going to try to improvise a tune to go along with the 12-bar blues, using the following notes:

C   D   E   G   A   B(**flat**)

- Ask the children to find these notes starting with a large bar marked C.

- Most of the class play the 12-bar blues pattern of chords while some individuals attempt to improvise above the chord pattern.
- There isn't any 'wrong' improvising; just some melodies that the children will agree sound better than others at certain points in the chord pattern.
- You could record the best pieces of improvising and make a blues piece.

Variation

- Once the class are happily playing their 12-bar blues pattern, you could record it several times to use as a backing track for the individuals doing their improvising. This way, the bulk of the class can listen and assess the improvising that is going on.

Cross-curricular links

Topic work – the children could write words on any topic to fit to their 12-bar blues improvising.
PSHE – 'ownership' of their improvisation, working as part of a team.
Maths – counting and patterns.

'Time for School'

Suitable for

KS1, KS2

Aims

- To develop the children's ability to keep several instrumental parts playing together.
- To encourage the use of alternate beaters on tuned percussion instruments.
- To involve a whole class in producing a piece of music.

Resources

- A copy of the 'Time for School' score
- A selection of tuned and untuned percussion instruments

What to do

- Write out the melody for the clock chiming in whatever way the children can follow it.
- The notes are all one-beat (crotchet) notes and follow a pattern.
- It would be possible to write it on a traditional stave with five lines and if necessary write the letter names of the notes underneath.
- If the children have tried Cabbage Patch Countdown (see p. 98) then they will be familiar with the stave notation.

B	G	A	D	D	A	B	G
B	G	A	D	D	A	B	G

- Ask a group of three or four children to keep this part playing at a very steady pace.
- A xylophone would be a good instrument to play this on.
- It is possible to have one group of children playing the first four notes and another group playing the second group of four notes.
- It is important to practise until the children are confident that they can keep this pattern going at a steady pace.

- Next add a speaking/chanting part that follows the school day with o'clock times, e.g.:

  Nine o'clock, start school
  Ten o'clock, break time
  Twelve o'clock, lunch time
  Three o'clock, home.

- This rhyme is chanted in time with the clock-chiming part.
- A third group of children could use claves or rhythm sticks to keep the ticking of the clock going and they would play:

  Rest   rest   click   click,   rest   rest   click   click.

- Try adding this part to the previous two parts.
- Finally, a group of children could play for the 'dong' of the clock.
- This could be played on a drum or cowbell.
- Put all four parts together and try to keep a very steady beat.

Variations

- Develop the chant by including other activities that happen at school or choose a different setting for the clock piece.
- For older children, the times could progress to more complicated times like 10.15 or 12.05.

Cross-curricular links

Maths – time skills, recognising patterns.
Language – telling the story of a school day or any day.
Topic work – this would connect with a topic on school, machines, people who help us, ourselves.

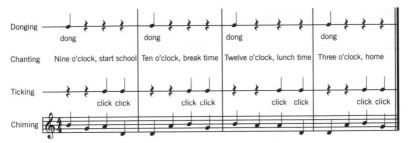

'Time for School'

'Moving House'

Suitable for

KS2

Aims

- To develop the children's reading skills using traditional stave notation.
- To encourage singing as part of a whole piece of music.
- To encourage some improvisation using untuned percussion during the rap part of the piece.

Resources

- A copy and/or recording of the song 'Moving House'
- A CD player
- A selection of tuned and untuned percussion instruments, with two matching beaters for each tuned percussion instrument

What to do

- Let the children listen to the recording of the song.
- Point out the different sections of the piece:
  - the instrumental part
  - the singing part
  - the rap part.

- Divide the class into those who will try playing the instrumental part and those who will use untuned percussion to accompany the rap section.
- Using the five lines and four spaces rhymes, go over the notes for the instrumental part making sure to point out the two sharps in the key signature – F# and C#. This means that any F or C notes are automatically sharp.

- The instrumental part is quite repetitive and could be divided up into three separate parts for small groups of children to play:

D D D D C# B A
E E E G F# G A
D D D D C# B A
C# B A G F# E D

- The group of children who are to accompany the rap section of the piece will need to discuss and try out various combinations of instruments until they are happy that the instruments will not drown out the speaking.
- Everyone can join in with the short singing section and in the speaking of the rap section.

Variation

- Have only one person on each instrumental part and one person speaking each verse of the rap section.

Cross-curricular links

Language – the difference between the singing section and the rapping section.
PSHE – being responsible for your own part, confidence building.
Topic work – would fit in well with a houses and homes project.

'Moving House'

1. Moving house can be a stressful time
Houses cost an awful lot of dimes!
Finding an estate agent, showing people round
Making sure another house can be found.

2. Careful with the mortgage, don't borrow too much
Just in case the interest rate goes right up.
Choose a good removal firm to move your stuff
Some are very careful, some are far too rough.

3. Just before you go – get your meter read.
Then pay your bill, yes that's what I said!
Lots of different things you will need to arrange
Just to make sure it's a very smooth change.

Twinkling Tumblers

Suitable for

KS1, KS2

Aims

- To allow the children to experiment and find out about sound production.
- To develop children's awareness of how high and low are affected by big and little.

Resources

- Eight glass tumblers
- A jug of water
- A beater or pencil
- A copy of the solfa staircase (see pp. 7, 8, 9)
- A selection of suitable songs/tunes, e.g.:

'Twinkle, Twinkle, Little Star' Doe doe so so la la so fa fa me me ray ray doe
So so fa fa me me ray So so fa fa me me ray
Doe doe so so la la so fa fa me me ray ray doe

'Frére Jacques' Doe ray me doe Doe ray me doe
Me fa so Me fa so
So la so fa me doe So la so fa me doe
Doe so doe Doe so doe

'Doe a Deer, a Female Deer' Doe ray me doe me doe me
Ray me fa fa me ray fa
Me fa so me so me so
Fa so la la so fa la

'Scotland the Brave' Doe doe ray me doe me so
High doe doe tee doe so me doe
Fa la fa me so me doe ray so la so
Doe doe ray me doe me so
High doe doe tee doe so me doe
Fa la fa me so me doe ray doe tee doe

What to do

- Ask the children to use the tumblers and water to produce a solfa staircase with eight notes in it.
- They will need to work out how much water to put into each tumbler in order to alter the note it can then produce when it is hit with the beater or pencil.
- Choose a song and try to play the song using the tumblers and beater.
- The solfa names will help the children to work out which tumbler they need to hit for the tune.
- You could put a card under each tumbler with the solfa name written on it in the correct colour.

Variation

- Ask the children to compose their own tunes and write them down using the solfa notation.

Cross-curricular links

Science – observing and recording experiments, investigating similarities and differences, does the sound get higher or lower as the glass fills?
PSHE – working as a team and relying on others.

Five·Finger Tunes

Suitable for

KS1, KS2

Aims

- To encourage greater confidence in playing on a keyboard.
- To help children develop dexterity when playing on a keyboard.

Resources

- As many keyboards as are available – it is possible to have two children sharing a keyboard.

What to do

- Ask all the children to put their right hand on the table and tap the table starting with their thumb as number 1 then fingers 2, 3, 4, ending with the pinkie on 5.
- Practise playing lots of different patterns using the numbers 1 to 5:

1 3 2 5 / 1 3 2 5	this is a four-beat pattern
1 2 3 / 5 4 3 / 1 2 3 / 5 4 3	this is a three-beat pattern
1 3 2 4 3 5 / 1 3 2 4 3 5	this is a six-beat pattern
1 2 3 4 5 / 5 4 3 2 1	this is a five-beat pattern.

- Let the children have as much practice at this as you can before letting them try the same thing on the keyboards.
- Make sure that their thumb (number 1) is placed on middle C on the keyboard.
- Ask the children to make up their own patterns and work out how many beats they have.

Variation

* Work out the fingering needed to play a well-known tune and write it up for the children to try on the keyboards, e.g.:

'When the Saints Go Marching In'
1 3 4 5 / 1 3 4 5 / 1 3 4 5 3 1 3 2 / 3 3 2 1 1 3 5 5 4 / 3 4 5 3 1 2 1

'Daddy's taking Us to the Zoo Tomorrow'
1 1 1 1 1 3 3 5 5 3 1 / 2 2 2 2 2 2 2 2 2 2 2 / 1 1 1 1 1 3 3 5 5 3 1 /
2 4 3 2 1
1 3 3 2 2 1 1 1 / 5 3 2 1 1 1 / 3 2 1 2 2 2 2 2 3 3 2 2 1 1 1

Cross-curricular links

Maths – counting, recognising patterns and following them.
PE – dexterity of movement with hands.

Chapter 3
Rhythm

Introduction

'All children and all adults are musical.' Janet Mills

All the activities in this section are trying to encourage the development of strong rhythmic skills and an in-built awareness and feeling of the pulse and beat in music. I usually ask children to think of the pulse in music in the same way as the pulse in our wrists. It is continuous and the beat is like our heartbeat – it can go faster and slower and in music we divide the beat in groups ranging from 2 to 12.

A lot of the games use the rhythms of taa, tate and a one-beat rest. A huge amount of useful work can be done using variations of these rhythms. Later, the two-beat note taa-aa is introduced.

The advanced activities in the Rhythm Section are:

- to encourage children to keep the beat but with more than one part of their body at a time.
- a rap to be spoken along with rhythmic accompaniment.
- asking children to play a scale with different rhythm patterns on each note.
- encouraging children to hear and feel the difference between four-beat notes and one-beat notes.
- asking the children to keep two or three different rhythmic parts going.
- and 30 are rhythmic performance pieces.

Clap a Rhyme

Suitable for

KS1

Aims

- To develop the children's listening skills in relation to rhythmic patterns.
- To develop inner hearing of a rhythmic pattern.
- To encourage the connection between a sound and a symbol.

Resources

- A list of well-known rhymes to clap the rhythm of, e.g.

  'Baa, Baa, Black Sheep'
  'Humpty Dumpty Sat on a Wall'
  'One, Two, Three, Four, Five, Once I Caught a Fish Alive'
  'Polly Put the Kettle On'
  'Hot Cross Buns'

What to do

- Make sure that the rhymes you are going to clap are familiar to the children, even going over them before starting the activity.
- Choose a rhyme and explain that instead of saying it you are going to clap it and the children should try to work out from your clapping which rhyme it is.
- Once they have guessed the rhyme, ask them to clap it with you saying the words to themselves as they go.
- Try starting off by saying a line of the rhyme then clapping the next line.
- Do this to the end of the rhyme.
- Then try clapping the first line, then saying a line until you reach the end of the rhyme.
- Ask a child if they can clap the whole rhyme whilst the rest of the class check they are clapping correctly.

Variation

- Try making a chart which includes some words of the rhyme and then a pictorial representation of what is being clapped, e.g., chart for 'One, Two, Three, Four, Five ...'

Cross-curricular links

Language – word patterns and syllables.
Art – pictorial representation of a nursery rhyme.

Pictorial Representation

Tell the Time Rhythms

Suitable for

KS1

Aims

- To encourage listening to distinguish rhythms that differ slightly from each other.
- To develop the use of taa, tate and a one beat rest.
- To use the game as an aid to learning how to tell the time.

Resources

- A large clock face with the designated rhythms on 12 cards that can be positioned beside a number on the clock face.
- Workcards of each rhythm or the 12 rhythms written up on the board.

What to do

- Go over each of the 12 rhythms.
- The leader should say the rhythms and ask the children to say them back.
- The leader should clap the rhythms and ask the children to clap them back.
- Once all 12 rhythms are known well, decide with the children where they should go on the clock. It might be simpler to keep the 'taa, taa, taa, taa' pattern for the number 12 so that it is easily recognisable as the 'o'clock' rhythm.
- Once the rhythms are all in place, the leader could start by clapping an o'clock time.
- Every o'clock time will end with 'taa, taa, taa, taa' and be prefaced with whatever rhythm is at the number chosen.
- It will take quite some time to build up the combination of recognising the rhythm and being able to tell the time the rhythms are saying.
- Depending on the stage of the children, you could introduce more complex times such as 2.20 or 4.35. The children would need to be clear about the fact that it would be the hour time that comes first, followed by the minutes.

> When there is a rest in the rhythm, it is useful to do an action to acknowledge the rest, for instance holding your hands flat out in front of you. This action can be done instead of saying 'rest' which somewhat cancels out the silence that a rest is.

Variations

- Instead of clapping, untuned percussion instruments could be used.
- Eventually, a child could clap or play the time and their classmates could guess with the child giving the correct answer being the next to be the leader.

Cross·curricular links

Maths – telling the time.
PSHE – working as part of a team and relying on other team members.

Concentration

Suitable for

KS2

Aims

- Encouraging counting the beat in your head.
- Extending memory capacity for rhythms.

Resources

- Prepare a list of potential rhythm patterns, e.g.:

  Zing, zing, dig a dig dig
  Hoopla, basket, in, out
  Slippy, slippy, slap, slap
  Wibble, wobble, zip-a-dee-doo
  Mega dish, hunky, give it a go

> **Basically, any combination of wacky word patterns will do – it's a good idea to have a bank of ideas in front of you if you are going to be the leader.**

What to do

- The leader says the rhythm pattern.
- The class think it to themselves and then say it out loud.
- Try several different rhythm patterns.
- Next time, the class do the same thing but the leader should say the next rhythm pattern while the class repeats the previous one.
- The class still have thinking time but as they repeat back the pattern, they have to also listen for the next rhythm pattern.
- Anyone who comes in at the wrong time or makes a mistake in the repeating of the words is 'out'!

Variation

- The class is divided into two groups and the leader feeds rhythms to two groups. This time the groups have to disregard what the other group are doing and concentrate on their own rhythm patterns – it's not easy!

It's essential to have quite a long list of potential rhythms ready.

Cross-curricular links

Topic work – ask the children to come up with rhythm patterns based on a specific one of their topics, e.g. space, dinosaurs, food.

Language – word patterns and alliteration could be used.

Maths – Lots of counting in your head and recognition of patterns and sequences.

Clap and Stamp and E-Ha!

Suitable for

KS1, KS2

Aims

- To hear and keep a beat.
- To sustain up to four different rhythmic parts playing together.
- To introduce a one-beat note (taa) and a one-beat rest.

Resources

- This activity is probably easier to do if the children are seated on chairs
- A class set of the clap/stamp sheet in A4 size
- A CD player with a lively **four-beat tune** which has a strong beat, e.g., any type of march played by a brass or military band, e.g., 'Come Follow the Band' from the musical *Barnum*

What to do

- Each child has the clap/stamp sheet in front of them with shoe, shoe, clap, clap at the top of the page.
- The class first say the sheet together after a count of four:

Shoe, shoe, clap, clap
Shoe, shoe, clap, clap
Shoe, clap, shoe, clap
Shoe, clap, clap, shoe.

- Next, repeat the whole sheet and say shoe but actually clap on the clap symbol.
- Next, repeat the whole sheet and tap your foot on the shoe symbol and clap on the clap symbol.
- When the class are ready, try this along with the recorded music.
- Play the music and practise counting 1 2 3 4 for a short time before attempting the whole sheet.
- When you reach the end of the pattern, just start again at the top.

Variations

- Turn the sheet to produce three more pieces of music:
  four shoes at the top:

  Shoe, shoe, shoe, shoe
  Clap, clap, shoe, shoe
  Clap, shoe, clap, clap
  Shoe, clap, clap, clap.

  Three hands at the top:
  Clap, clap, clap, shoe
  Clap, clap, shoe, clap
  Shoe, shoe, clap, clap
  Shoe, shoe, shoe, shoe.

  Upside down:
  Shoe, clap, clap, shoe
  Clap, shoe, clap, shoe
  Clap, clap, shoe, shoe
  Clap, clap, shoe, shoe.

- Divide the class into two and have two parts playing at the same time.
- Divide the class into three or four groups.
- Make 'shoe' a rest (ssh instead of shoe) and you have four more pieces of music.
- Substitute untuned percussion instruments for shoe and clap, e.g.: shoe – woodblock; clap – tambourine
- Each variation could have a different set of instruments.

Cross-curricular links

Whatever topic is being covered, an appropriate piece of music can be chosen, e.g.:

- Ancient Egypt: 'Walk Like an Egyptian', The Bangles.
- Space: 'It's the Final Countdown', Europe.

PSHE – team building, working together.
Maths – counting, recognising and sustaining patterns.

Candle Game

Suitable for

KS1, KS2

Aims

- To encourage the keeping of a **pulse**.
- To develop the skill of keeping a rhythm in time with the beat.
- To encourage teambuilding/working together.

Resources

- Space for a circle
- Minimum of six participants – no maximum limit
- Willingness to sing unaccompanied
- A copy of the song 'Glowing Candle Light'

What to do

- Make a circle with the participants.
- One person is in the middle – they are the candle and they dip their knees when everyone blows.
- One half of the circle keeps a pulse by tapping onto their hands. There are four beats in each bar.
- The other half of the circle use rhythm sticks/claves to tap the rhythm of the words:

G	G	G	A	G		
So	so	so	la	so		
Glowing		candle		light	(blow)	

G	G	G	A	G		
So	so	so	la	so		
Warm	and	cheerful		sight	(blow)	

G	G	G	A	G	F	E	D
So	so	so	la	so	fa	me	ray
See	the	candle		burning		brightly	

E E	D	D	C	
Me me	ray	ray	doe	
Shining	in	the	night	(blow)

Variations

- Once the pattern is established, the person in the middle identifies a new candle person and takes over their job.
- The two halves can swap jobs each time or to make it slightly harder, alternate people in the circle can do the pulse keeping or the rhythm playing.

Cross·curricular links

Topic work – make up a rhyme connected to the topic being studied, e.g. space: the person in the middle is the rocket that shoots up into the sky on 'blast':

Rocket standing by (blast)
Wait to shoot up high (blast)
Check ignition, now for take-off
Powering through the sky (blast).

PSHE – working as a team, changing responsibilities.

Rhythm Banking

Suitable for

KS1, KS2

Aims

- To develop use of rhythm patterns.
- To encourage rhythmic and melodic invention in music making.
- To aid development of a class topic.
- To intoduce **grid notation**.

Resources

- Cards with **taa** (a **crotchet** or one-beat note) tate (two **quavers** or half-beat notes) taa-aa (a **minim** or two-beat note) rhythms on them.
- A card with a one-beat rest on it.
- The title of the topic being studied by the class.

What to do

- To obtain the initial list of words associated with the topic, brainstorming is probably best. Making a long list on the board and then working out the rhythms of the words means everyone is included.
- If we take space as our topic, the list could be, e.g.

  rocket, moon, spaceship, astronaut, gravity, atmosphere, take-off, countdown, launch pad, lunar module, oxygen, pod, go exploring, air, universal, bounce.

- Once the list is made, each word needs to be put into a rhythm category.
- The class can then be divided into groups for each rhythm category, and each group should play or clap only when their rhythm appears.
- The words are then written out in a **grid notation** (see below, p. 164).
- Each group could choose an instrument for their rhythm and play the grid using these instruments.

Variations

- A scale of C could be played ascending/descending across the grid:

Astronaut on C
Spaceship on D
Go exploring on E
Moon on F
Air on G
Atmosphere on A
Countdown on B
Universal on high C

High C on launch pad
B on oxygen
A on lunar module
G on pod
F on rocket
E on take off
D on gravity
C on bounce.

- For further composing, the C pentatonic scale could be used: C D E G A.
- To start with, limit the notes to E and G; then try E, G and A.
- Try composing melodies using C D E G and A.

Cross-curricular links

Topic work – topic-related vocabulary.
Language – syllables, stress of words.
PSHE – working as a team, cooperation.

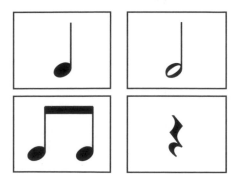

Astronaut	spaceship	go exploring	moon
Air	atmosphere	countdown	universal
Launch pad	oxygen	lunar module	pod
Rocket	take-off	gravity	bounce

♩ ♩

rocket
spaceship
take-off
countdown
launch pad

♫ ♩

astronaut
gravity
atmosphere
oxygen

♩

moon
pod
air
bounce

♫ ♫

lunar module
go exploring
universal

Be a Square

Suitable for

KS1, KS2

Aims

- To introduce grid notation.
- To encourage counting and playing to a beat.
- To develop skills of inventing.

Resources

- Some prepared grids: Eight squares in a line and numbered 1–8 (see below)
  2 × 8 squares, one under the other (see below)
  4 × 8 squares, labelled with instrument choices (32 squares)
  4 × 8 squares with instrument pictures in the boxes (32 squares)
- CDs with music that has a strong beat for backing

What to do

- Give the children an eight-square grid and ask them to put a cross in four of the squares.
- Counting steadily from 1 to 8 the children can perform their grid by clapping when there is a cross and making some kind of movement with their hands for the empty space – this will help keep the timing accurate.
- The children then choose a different symbol and add another action to their grid, e.g.

  X = clapping
  O = clicking fingers
  ~ = patting knees.

- The children can then perform their own grid, which involves the accurate reading of two different actions within an eight-beat grid.

- In pairs or groups, the children can join two grids together and perform them with the body percussion actions.
- If each group uses different body percussion, the piece can quickly become quite complex.

Variations

- Use a 4 × 8-square grid and have a line for each different body percussion, e.g.,

Line 1 = clapping
Line 2 = finger clicking
Line 3 = patting knees
Line 4 = stamping

- Use a 4 × 8-square grid and have pictures of the action to be done in the squares chosen.
- In some squares there may be two pictures, which would indicate a double clap or click or whatever action is required.

Cross-curricular links

Maths – counting, following patterns.
Language – various ways of reading and following a line of information.
PSHE – working as part of a team.

1	2	3	4	5	6	7	8

Grid with 4 × 8 squares

Press Plastic

Suitable for

KS1, KS2

Aims

- To encourage rhythmic movement in time to a beat.
- To encourage teamwork to achieve a whole class rhythmic movement.

Resources

- A plastic cup for each person taking part
- A CD of fairly slow and steady backing music, e.g., Abba's 'Thank You for the Music' or Paul McCartney's 'Frog Chorus'
- A CD player

What to do

- Everyone sits in a circle, close enough to hold hands with the people on either side.
- Introduce several instructions:
  – clap – clap your hands in front of you
  – push – push both hands out in front of you (like pushing a piece of furniture away from you).
- Now try keeping a beat and getting everyone to go clap, push, clap, push in time to the beat.
- Now continue with the instructions and add:
  – sides – use both your hands to clap the hands of the people on either side of you.
- The best way to do this is to ask the children to clap then sides.
- Start very slowly and gradually speed up.
- Having mastered these three instructions put them together and try: clap, push, clap, sides.
- Put on the music and try doing this pattern then resting for four beats and doing the pattern again.

- Once this has been mastered, introduce the plastic cup and try the instructions:

  – lift – pass.

- This involves lifting the plastic cup up with the right hand and passing it to the person on your right.
- Practise doing this to a beat and then to the music.
- Once all of the instructions have been mastered, join them together:

  clap, push, clap, sides
  clap, push, lift, pass.

- Try to do this to a beat and then to the music.
- When you add the music, leave a four- or eight-beat rest between each pattern.

Variations

- Change the direction of the cup moving.
- Have the cup move right and left alternately, e.g.

  clap, push, clap, sides
  clap, push, lift, pass (to the right)
  clap, push, clap, sides
  clap, push, lift, pass (to the left)

- Use faster music for the backing track!

Cross-curricular links

Maths – patterns and sequences.
PSHE – coordination and teamwork.
PE – movement as part of a team.

'Drunken Sailor' Drumming

Suitable for

KS1, KS2

Aim

- To encourage the children to hear and feel the difference between pulse and rhythm.

Resources

- Children and space

What to do

- Sing through a verse and chorus of 'What Shall We Do with the Drunken Sailor' with the whole class.
- Sing through again, but this time ask everyone to keep a pulse by gently patting on their knees.
- It can be quite useful to talk about the pulse that every human being has and the fact that music has exactly the same kind of a pulse.
- Sing through again, but this time ask everyone to gently tap out the rhythm of the words, with a tap for every syllable.
- Once this has been done, ask everyone to stand in a circle all facing the back of the person next to them.
- Sing through the song again and this time tap the pulse on the shoulders of the person in front of you.
- Now try, in silence, to tap the rhythm of the words on the shoulders of the person in front of you.
- Finally, try the activity in pairs: sit facing your partner and while one child taps out the pulse on their partner's knees, the other child taps out the rhythm of the words on their partner's shoulders.
- Singing at the same time as trying to do this partner work is quite difficult, so a recording of the song could be used or having a piano player play the song would work also.

Variations

- Use a different, but equally well-known, song.
- Instead of tapping the pulse on your knees, keep the pulse with your feet.

Cross-curricular links

Language – finding out about syllables in words.
PSHE – coordination (keeping more than one action going at the same time); team work and partner work.

Tap it Out and Pass it On

Suitable for

KS1, KS2

Aims

- To encourage listening and retention of a rhythm.
- To increase confidence in playing untuned percussion instruments.
- To develop the children's skills in reproducing a rhythm.

Resources

- A set of cards with a selection of rhythms (with or without words to aid the memory)

What to do

- Go over each rhythm card with the class and make sure everyone knows how to tap out the rhythms.
- Divide the class into two teams and ask them to number themselves.
- Ask the children to spread themselves out in a large hall with their numbers all muddled up.
- Ask the number one person in each team to come individually and look at one of the rhythm cards. (It is probably best to give each team a different rhythm.)
- The number one person then has to tap the rhythm they have been allocated to person number two in their team.
- Person number two passes it on to person number three and so on until the last person in the team has received it.
- Both teams should do this at the same time, but with different rhythms.
- Once the last person in each team has received their rhythm, they tap it out for the whole team to hear and compare how accurate it is compared to the rhythm card they started with.

Obviously, the rhythms should be set at a level suitable for the children taking part in the game.

Variations

- You could introduce tuned percussion instruments and ask the team to pass on a melody rather than a rhythm.
- Eventually, you could ask the team to pass on a melody that includes rhythm.

Cross-curricular links

Language – making up little rhymes to help with remembering the rhythms.
PSHE – working as part of a team. What one person in the team does has an effect on the whole team, as well as an effect on the outcome of the game.
Topic work – the rhythms for tapping out could have words connected with a topic the class are studying.

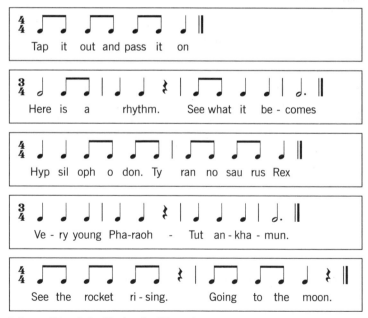

Tap it Out and Pass it On Rhythm Card Exemplars

Off Beat/On Beat

Suitable for

KS1, KS2

Aims

- To help the children to hear and feel an **off-beat** note and an **on-beat** note
- To develop the children's ability to keep one rhythmic pattern going whilst another is playing.

Resources

- A backing track that is in four beats, something jazzy would be good, e.g., any ragtime piece or military band marching music
- A CD player

What to do

- Ask the children to pat their knees and then clap their hands alternately:

  X   X   X   X   X   X   X   X
  Knees, clap, knees, clap, knees, clap, knees, clap!

- Next ask the children to do the action of patting their knees but not make an actual sound and still continue with the hand clapping as before:

  Rest   X   rest   X   rest   X   rest   X
          Clap   clap   clap   clap

- Once the children have practised both versions a few times, put on the backing track you have chosen and count them in (1 2 3 4) to first do the knee, clap routine.
- At an agreed signal, change to the off-beat clapping using the silent knee tap to help get the claps in the correct place.

Variations

- Try different body percussion to achieve the same end result, e.g., pat cheeks then click fingers; or tap nose then stamp feet.
- Once you have introduced a few different versions you could have the class divided into however many groups are required and use all the different versions together.

Cross-curricular links

Maths – counting and recognising patterns.
PE – movement and coordination.
PSHE – body awareness.

Sounds and Silence

Suitable for

KS1, KS2

Aims

- To develop the children's awareness of how silence is part of music.
- To give children opportunities to both play and create silence.
- To extend the children's listening skills.

Resources

- Three or four different percussion instruments that will be difficult to keep silent when passing from one person to another, e.g., maraca, tambourine, sleigh bells, Indian bells
- Background music that has a fairly clear beat – some party tracks would be ideal

What to do

- Have the children sitting in a circle and explain that they are going to play a game similar to 'Pass the parcel', but they are going to pass rhythms and silences.
- Distribute the percussion instruments around the circle and ask each child holding one to play you a stated rhythm, e.g., taa, taa, tate, taa.
- Check that everyone in the circle is clear about the rhythm they are being asked to copy.
- Start the backing music and ask each child to play the rhythm on their instrument and then pass it to the next person, who plays the rhythm, and so on.
- When the music is stopped and there is silence, the instrument has to be passed silently to the next person until the music restarts and the rhythm is continued.

Variations

- If there are four instruments being passed around, allocate a different rhythm to each instrument and ask each child to play the rhythm associated with the instrument they receive.
- It is probably best to start off this version with only two different instruments and rhythms and gradually build up to three and then four.

Cross-curricular links

PSHE – develops individual and group listening and sharing.
Language – listening and repeating rhythm patterns.

Rhythm Around

Suitable for

KS1, KS2

Aims

- To develop the skill of composing and copying a rhythmic pattern.
- To encourage listening skills.

Resources

- A single beater and a woodblock
- A backing track that has a jaunty beat
- A CD player

What to do

- Have the children sitting in a circle and, as they pass the beater from one to the next, ask them to chant:

  Pass the beater round and round
  Listen to the rhythmic sound.

- As this is happening, have the backing track playing and ask the children to pass the beater in time to the music.
- It is probably best to state which hand everyone has to use to pass the beater, e.g., all move your right hand from right to left all the time so that when the beater comes to you, you just pass it in time with the music.
- After several times of passing the beater, a child chooses to play a rhythm on the woodblock.
- This rhythm has to be in time with the backing track, e.g., tate, tate, tate, taa.
- As soon as the rhythm has been tapped out on the woodblock, the rest of the circle should clap it as an echo.
- The chant then continues and the beater is passed around again until another person tries tapping out a rhythm on the woodblock.

Variation

• Instead of a child playing the rhythm on the woodblock, the leader of the group could clap a rhythm and whoever has the beater at that time has to copy the rhythm on the woodblock.

Cross-curricular links

Language – feeling the rhythm of sound helps in the speaking of poetry or prose. Topic work – the rhythm being played could be set to words appropriate to the topic being studied, e.g., 'Tutankhamun died very, very young'; or 'There's no gravity on the moon'.

Happy Music

Suitable for

KS1, KS2

Aims

- To develop the children's ability to play a four-beat rhythm in time with the beat.
- To encourage the skill of following a conductor
- To widen the children's knowledge of untuned percussion instruments

Resources

- A wide selection of untuned percussion instruments
- Enough of each instrument for a group of four or five children to have one each
- A recording of some happy sounding music with two, three or four beats in a bar, e.g.:

Theme from *Barnum*
'Potato Head Blues' (Louis Armstrong)
Theme from *Match of the Day*
Any bright, happy music.

What to do

- Ask the children to name as many untuned percussion instruments as they can (any percussion instruments that cannot play a tune).
- Start with one instrument and give a group of children a four-beat rhythm to play:

  Tambourine – taa, taa, tate, taa – play the tambourine.

- The words are to help the children remember what their rhythm is.
- Eventually, every child will be part of a group, so in a class of 30 there could be six groups with five children in each or ten groups with three children in each.

- Have different rhythms for each instrument, e.g.:

  Maracas – tate, taa, tate, taa – shake it here, shake it there
  Sleigh bells – tate, tate, taa, taa – jingle, jingle sleigh bells
  Guiros – taa, taa, taa, tate – one, two, three, guiro
  Triangles – tate, tate, tate, taa – 'Twinkle, Twinkle, Little Star'
  Indian bells – tate, taa, taa, taa – Indian bells, ting, ting
  Rhythm sticks – taa, tate, tate, taa – we play the rhythm sticks
  Drums – taa, taa, rest, rest.

- Once the children are all confident at playing their group's rhythm, the conductor stands at the front and points to the group they want to play.
- Each group only plays for four beats so they only play their part once.
- The conductor must be ready to move quickly from one group to the next.
- Every group has to watch and listen as they don't know when they will be asked to play.

Variations

- A child can become the conductor.
- The rhythm can be extended to be an eight-beat rhythm.
- Try a piece in three beats.

Cross-curricular links

PSHE – working as part of a team, listening to others.
Maths – counting whilst playing and also keeping time when waiting for your own turn.

Boom Cha Cha

Suitable for

KS1, KS2

Aims

- To develop the children's awareness of beat and in particular three beats in a bar.
- To encourage the use of rhythm patterns within a song.
- To encourage the use of instrumental rhythm patterns within a song.

Resources

- A selection of percussion instruments
- A few well-known songs that have three beats in a bar:

  'My Bonnie Lies Over the Ocean'
  'Edelweiss'
  'Oh My Little Augustine'
  'Clementine'
  'The Red Yoyo'

What to do

- Use the words 'Boom Cha Cha' to help the children clap the rhythm.
- Try asking them to pat their knees on 'Boom' and clap on 'Cha Cha'.
- Ask the children to sing one of the listed songs.
- Once they are confident with the singing, ask them to sing and do the 'Boom Cha Cha' rhythm at the same time.
- The 'Boom' should land on the first beat of each bar with the 'Cha, Cha' on beats two and three.
- Once the children feel confident doing this, add percussion instruments in place of the knee patting and clapping, e.g., have a drum play on the 'Boom' and a tambourine on the 'Cha Cha'.
- To start with use only two children for the instrumental playing and gradually add more to each group.

> It is much harder to play only part of the rhythmic pattern and sing at the same time.

Variations

- Ask the children to pair up and do a knee slap, hand clap then slap each other's hands for beat three:

  slap, clap, together
  for beats one, two, three.

- After singing the song with these paired actions, the pairs could organise their instruments for an instrumental version.

Cross-curricular links

Maths – counting and recognising patterns.
PE – movement and coordination.
PSHE – working as part of a team, body awareness, confidence building.

Ten Good Men

Suitable for

KS1, KS2

Aims

- To encourage the children to concentrate and remember a sequence of sounds.
- To develop the children's listening skills.
- To develop the use of body percussion when playing rhythmic patterns.

Resources

- A large space – enough for a group of 30 children to stand in a circle

What to do

- Ask the children to number themselves around the circle from one to ten.
- Once ten is reached start again at number one.
- Start by practising counting steadily around the circle – if helpful, the leader could keep a beat on a drum or tambourine.
- Once the children are counting steadily, decide on a sound that will be made in place of saying number one, e.g., clap.
- Continue counting steadily, but instead of saying one, the child just claps.
- Now choose another number to substitute a sound for, e.g., six = click fingers.
- Continue counting around the circle, but this time there is no number one or number six; instead there is a clap and a click.
- Continue to choose a number at random and ask the children to come up with body percussion possibilities.
- Eventually, there is no counting using numbers, but only a series of sounds, e.g.:

  Clap, sniff, slap knees, stamp, wiggle tongue, click, pat cheeks, 'ooh', rub hands, 'eeeh'.

- Once the children are confident with this sequence, you can gradually speed up the beat!

Variation

- For very confident groups, once the pattern is established, ask all the number ones to swap with all the number sevens. They have to be ready to perform the sound for their new number. Gradually swap everyone over!

Cross-curricular links

Maths – counting, recognising patterns and adjusting to changes in them.
PE – movement and coordination.

Rhythm Hot Plates

Suitable for

KS1, KS2

Aims

- To develop the children's awareness of different rhythm patterns.
- To increase the children's confidence in using the rhythms taa, tate and taa-a.

Resources

- Have four paper plates for each child or group of children
- Each plate has a rhythm written at the top of it with a word that fits to that rhythm, e.g.:

  A two-beat note (taa-a) – a note that is not coloured in – with the word 'bread' written below it.
  Tate, taa with the words 'apple pie' written below it
  Tate, tate with the words 'mince and tatties' written below it.
  Taa, taa with the words 'ice cream' written below it.

What to do

- Ask the children to have a look at each plate and then have a brainstorming session to list as many foods as you can which would fit into one of the categories, e.g.:

  Sausages, pizza, fish and chips, honey sandwich, hot dogs, stew, macaroni, haggis, treacle sponge, chips, chicken nuggets, fairy cakes, etc.

- Ask everyone in the group to put all the items in the list on to the correct plate.

Variations

- A fifth plate with the rhythm taa, tate could be added for such foods as fish fingers, sliced melon, fruit yoghurt.
- Once the foods have all been allocated to a plate, the children in the group have to see how many extra foods they can add to their plates.

Cross-curricular links

Language – syllables and patterns in words.
Topic work – this activity could link to a topic on food and could be adapted for most topics, e.g.:
    Pyramids instead of plates for Ancient Egypt
    Spaceships for space
    Cars for transport, etc.

Conducting Capers

Suitable for

KS1, KS2

Aims

- To encourage children to learn how to **conduct** two, three and four beats in a bar.
- To give the children an opportunity to try to hear the difference between different time signatures.

Resources

- A copy of the conducting patterns sheet
- A selection of music for the children to conduct to – dance music (sometimes in two beats), waltzes (three beats), marches (usually in four beats)

What to do

- Take one type of conducting at a time.
- It is probably best to start with two beats, then three beats and end with four beats.
- Practise conducting two beats whilst counting 1, 2.
- Make sure the down beat is always on the count of 1.
- Play a piece with two beats and ask the children to conduct in time with the music.
- Practise conducting three beats whilst counting 1, 2, 3, making sure the down beat is always on the count of 1.
- Play a piece with three beats and ask the children to conduct in time with the music.
- Practise conducting four beats whilst counting 1, 2, 3, 4, making sure the down beat is always on the count of 1.
- Play a piece with four beats and ask the children to conduct in time with the music.

Variations

- Once the children are confident with their conducting, you could play a piece of music and ask them to work out how many beats there are.
- When they have successfully worked out the number of beats, they could conduct the piece using the correct movements.

Cross·curricular link

Maths – counting and following a pattern.

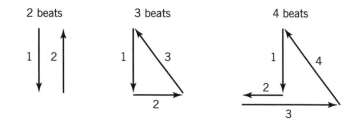

Conducting Patterns

Rhythm Ostinati

Suitable for

KS1, KS2

Aims

- To develop the children's ability to maintain more than one rhythmic part within a group.
- To encourage group rhythmic work.
- To introduce the term **ostinato**.

Resources

- A selection of untuned percussion instruments, e.g. maracas, rhythm sticks and tambours
- A copy of the Rhythm Ostinati sheet for each child (please note that the ostinati on this sheet all have four beats in a bar. The ostinati could be made up in three or five beats in a bar)

What to do

- Ask the children to read the rhythms on the Rhythm Ostinati sheet by using the words taa, tate and ssh for rest.
- Next, ask the children to clap each of the rhythms.
- First, divide the class into two groups, then ask the first group to clap rhythm number one.
- Ask the second group to clap rhythm number two.
- Ask both groups to clap at the same time, making sure that they listen to each other to hear how their own part fits with the other part.
- Divide the class into three groups and ask each group to clap their rhythm then add the three parts together.
- Once the children are confident with the clapping parts, choose instruments for each group and have the maraca group, the rhythm stick group and the tambour group.

Obviously, the more parts there are, the greater the difficulty.

Variations

- Once the children have tried all the ostinati on the sheet, they could make up their own rhythm ostinato and try to perform a piece with several ostinati playing together.
- The children could make up little rhymes to help them remember what their rhythm is.

Cross-curricular links

Maths – recognising and continuing patterns.
Language – making up rhymes to match with a rhythm, syllables in words.

Rhythm Ostinati Sheet

Slap, Clap, Say your Word

Suitable for

KS1, KS2

Aims

- To encourage the children to feel the pulse or beat of the music.
- To give children the opportunity to insert their own rhythm into a group composition.

Resources

- A selection of untuned percussion instruments

What to do

- Ask the children to sit in a circle and count a steady 1, 2, 3, 4 for a few seconds.
- Next ask the children to pat their knees twice on 1, 2 and then tap two fingers on their hand on beats 3 and 4.
- The leader of the group should then insert a word, e.g., towns in Scotland: Aberdeen, Edinburgh, Glasgow, Dundee, Perth, etc.
- The leader says their town on the two lap beats and the class echo the town on the two hand taps.
- Do this until the class are quite skilled at getting their echo exactly in time with the beat.
- Once the children are confident with this, try moving the game around the circle.
- In this version, an individual child says the town name on the knees and there is silence on the hand taps.
- Each child takes it in turn to say their town on the knee pats and everyone keeps time by doing the hand taps.

Variation

- Each child claps the name of another child in the circle which then dictates where the game moves to around the circle. Whichever child's name is said then has to take their turn next.

Cross-curricular links

Topic work – this would work with any topic and would reinforce all the work done in class.

Language – vocabulary and fitting a certain number of syllables into a space.

Match the Rhythm

Suitable for

KS1, KS2

Aims

- To develop the children's awareness of rhythm patterns.
- To develop the children's ability to recognise and match specific rhythmic patterns.

Resources

- A large selection of phrases that match with rhythms using taa and tate
- A selection of untuned percussion instruments

What to do

- With children who are familiar with the taa and tate rhythms, show at first three rhythm patterns and three sets of words:

I love fish and chips	x x	x x	x x	X
Ice cream is my favourite treat	x x	X	x x	X
Brussel sprouts make me sick	X	X	x x	X

- The children have to say the phrases, clap the rhythms and then sort out which rhythm matches with which set of words.

Variations

- The children could make up the word phrases and write down the appropriate rhythms.
- For any topic, the phrases could reflect what the children have learned about their topic.

Cross-curricular links

Language – syllables, word patterns and stresses.
Topic work – can link with any topic.
Maths – problem solving, recognising patterns.

Notation

'Ugly Bug Ball'

Suitable for

KS1, KS2

Aims

- To encourage the children to use the rhythms taa, tate and tai-fe.
- To encourage the children to play untuned percussion instruments.
- To develop the children's sense of beat.

Resources

- A copy of the 'Ugly Bug Ball' music
- A board on which to write the various percussion parts
- Some untuned percussion instruments – maracas, rhythm sticks and tambourines
- A recording of the 'Ugly Bug Ball' by Burl Ives
- A CD player

What to do

- Let the children hear the recording and encourage them to join in with the **chorus**, perhaps even making up actions.
- Start with the maraca part and point out that it uses only tate rhythms.
- The two lines and two dots at the end of the parts are called a **repeat sign** and mean that the part has to be repeated. Make sure the children realise this so that their part will fit with the music.
- Point out that the rhythm stick part uses only taa notes, so will be slower than the maraca part.
- Point out that the tambourine part uses the rhythms tai-fe, tai-fe, taa and fits with that part of the recorded music.
- The maracas and rhythm sticks play during the verses and the tambourines play during the **instrumentals**.
- The children can sing the words of the chorus.
- Once all the parts have been practised individually, the class can play and sing along with the recording.

Variation

- Actions could be added to the chorus to make a mini dance routine which is done in strict time with the music.

Cross-curricular links

Maths – counting and continuing patterns.
Topic – would fit with a study of mini-beasts.

Introduction – count 1–8   1–4

Verse 1   maracas

rhythm sticks

Chorus   Come on let's crawl, gotta crawl, gotta crawl
To the Ugly Bug Ball, to the Ball, to the Ball
And a happy time we'll have there
One and all at the Ugly Bug Ball

Instrumental   tambourines

count 1–9

count 1–8   1–8

Verse 2
Chorus

Instrumental   tambourines

count 1–8   1–8

1 2 3 4 5 6 7 8 9 10 11 12

Verse 3
Chorus

'Ugly Bug Ball'

3, 4 and 5

Suitable for

KS1, KS2

Aims

- To introduce time signatures in 3, 4 and 5 beats in a bar.
- To increase the children's confidence in making up rhythms to a beat.

Resources

- A board on which to write a variety of rhythm patterns using 3, 4 and 5 beats in a bar (see below)

What to do

- Ask the children to look at one of the rhythm patterns and count while they clap the taa notes and don't clap on the rests.
- Do the same with the three examples using only taa notes and rests.
- Next move on and try the examples with tate notes included in the rhythms.
- Let individuals try clapping the rhythms as well giving opportunities for the whole class to clap together.
- Tell the children that the numbers at the beginning of the music are the time signature.
- The top number tells you the number of beats in each bar.
- The bottom number tells you the type of beat and a number four tells you that the beat is a crotchet or taa beat. Therefore, each beat is worth one count.

Variations

- Ask the children to choose one of the time signatures and make up their own rhythmic pattern using taa, tate and rests.
- For some extension work, older children could introduce more complex rhythms, e.g., tafatefe (four **semiquavers** or quarter-beat notes drawn with two lines across the top).

Cross-curricular links

Maths – dividing up the beats in a bar, recognising patterns, counting.

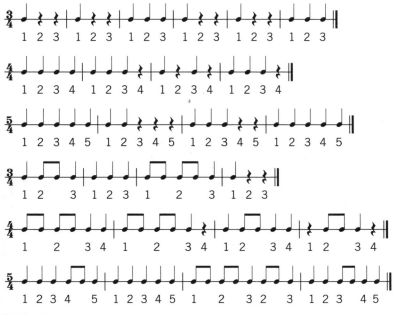

Rhythm Patterns

Advanced

Beat Box Body

Suitable for

KS2

Aim

- To develop 2-, 3- and 4-way independence in keeping a rhythm.

Resources

- CD player
- A selection of current chart CDs with a steady four beats per bar and moderate tempo

What to do

- Tap toes in time with the music, right and left.
- Clap in time with the music 1 2 3 4.
- Clap only on beats 1 and 3, then try only 2 and 4.
- Try tapping feet and clapping patterns together.
- Try tapping 1 2 3 4 and clapping quavers/half beat notes, i.e., two notes on beats 2 and 4.

- Slap beats 1 2 3 4 on the right thigh.
- Keep that going but add a slap on the left thigh on beat 3.
- Keep that going and add a stamp on beat 1 with the right foot.

- Do the foot tapping with your right foot in front of your left foot about a stride apart and rock backwards and forwards.
- Add in the clapping as before on beats 2 and 4.
- Try adding the left hand, tapping your thigh on beat 3.

Variation

- As many permutations as can be thought out using clapping, feet tapping, leg slapping, shoulder tapping using the right hand to tap the left shoulder or the left hand to tap the right shoulder.

Cross-curricular links

PSHE – coordination.
Maths – counting, sequences.

'Digestive System Rap'

Suitable for

KS1, KS2

Aims

- To develop the feeling of a pulse and playing instruments to a beat.
- To encourage the composing of words for a specific topic.
- To learn about the workings of the digestive system.

Resources

- A copy of the 'Digestive System Rap' for each member of the class (see p. 204)
- A wide selection of percussion instruments
- A diagram of the digestive system (available to download from the website)

%What to do

- The letters in **RAP** stand for rhythmically accentuated poetry, and as such, the object of this activity is to add suitable rhythm to accentuate the poem about the digestive system, making the poem into a rap.
- Discuss the diagram of the digestive system (p. 204) and find out what each of the individual parts do.
- Read through the rap making sure that there is a steady beat as you do so – perhaps tapping a beat with your hand on the table.
- Take a verse at a time and decide which percussion instruments are most appropriate for the part of the digestive system being mentioned.

- **Verse 1** – rhythm sticks would be good for starting the keeping of the beat. Decide how many clicks you want to do before you start saying the verse and keep the rhythm sticks playing until the end of the verse.
- On the last line, you could add an ascending glissando (slide the beater on a glockenspiel or xylophone from the largest bar to the smallest bar) to indicate the food going off!

- **Verse 2** – a two-tone woodblock could be used to provide the beat this time and continue through the verse with a descending glissando for after the last line.
- **Verse 3** – guiros could keep the beat to represent the churning of the stomach.
- When the second line is said, there could be a **discordant** sound for the acid part of the story – playing the notes G and A together at the top end of the instrument would work well for this.
- **Verse 4** – maracas could keep the beat this time and perhaps have a rain-stick playing throughout the verse to represent the blood flowing through the digestive system.
- **Verse 5** – Indian bells could keep the beat to try and indicate the water in the system.
- A swannee whistle could play at selected parts, e.g., 'Ain't it clever, ain't it good.'
- **Verse 6** – a cabasa could be used for the beat to indicate the squeezing muscles.
- After the last line, the class could use their voices to make an 'uh!' sound to finish off the whole digestive process!

Variations

- There are unlimited variations as everyone will have their own ideas for which instruments/sounds are suitable for telling the story of the digestive system.
- It is possible to decide on simply having a continuous beat throughout the rap and say the words to the beat without adding any other instruments.

Cross-curricular links

Topic work – a rap could be written for any topic being studied.
Language – discussion of suitable words, stresses required, construction of a poem.

'The Digestive System Rap'

1. **Mouth** – teeth cut and grind
   Mix food with saliva
   Starch digestion starts you know
   Eat that food now off we go.

2. In the **oesophagus** – peristalsis
   Waves of muscle action.
   Keeps that food a-moving
   Down that tube a-grooving.

3. **Stomach** churns and squashes food
   and produces acid
   which kills bacteria and also starts
   all of the digestion part.

4. **Liver** changes nutrients
   Into useful forms
   Pancreas – enzymes
   Duodenum – mixes
   Bloodstream delivers all the
   Body's little fixes.

5. **Colon** can absorb water
   And also minerals
   Ain't it clever, ain't it good
   To take them from digested food.

6. **Rectum** muscles squeeze.
   The undigested food into faeces.
   Time for them to leave
   Ready, steady, squeeze!

Frozen Food

Suitable for

KS1, KS2

Aims

- To encourage the recognition of rhythms using taa and tate.
- To use taa and tate rhythms in the playing of a scale.

Resources

- A copy of the song for every child
- A CD player
- A recording of the song
- A tuned percussion instrument for every two children
- Two matching beaters for each instrument

What to do

- Listen to the song and then sing it.
- Say and then clap the rhythms of all the foods mentioned in the song.
- Give every child responsibility for one of the foods mentioned.
- Sing the song again and ask the children to clap, as well as sing, when the food they have been allocated is mentioned.
- Next, ask the children to notice that the second half of the song is actually an ascending scale of C using the rhythms of the food.
- Ask the children to play the notes on their tuned percussion:

Pizza, pizza, pizza, pizza – C C, C C, C C, C C
chips, chips, chips, chips – D, D, D, D
frozen fish, frozen fish – E E E, E E E
chicken nuggets, chicken nuggets – F F F F, F F F F
ice cream, ice cream – G G G G
apple pie, apple pie – A A A, A A A
pizza, pizza, pizza, pizza – B B, B B, B B, B B
chips, chips, chips, chips – C, C, C, C

- Ask the children to tell you if there are any foods which have the same rhythm pattern (frozen fish and apple pie are the only two).
- Sing the song and play along with the second half of the song. You could end with a play list of all the foods available in the freezer.

Variations

- Compose some rhythm patterns using only the foods in the freezer.
- You could choose some notes from the scale of C to add a tune to your rhythm pattern.

Cross-curricular links

Topic work – fits with a topic about food.

Language – extracting the information you need from a piece of writing; revision of syllables.

'**Frozen Food**'

Taste and Hear the Difference

Suitable for

KS1, KS2

Aims

- To develop the skill of hearing the difference between the length of notes.
- To encourage active listening.
- To develop playing skills using alternate beaters.

Resources

- A copy of the song for each child
- A recording of the song
- A CD player
- A tuned percussion instrument for every two children
- Two matching beaters for each instrument

What to do

- Let the children hear the song.
- Ask the children to notice the music at the end of the song. (Music played at the end of a song is called a coda.)
- There are fast notes and slow notes at the end of the song.
- The fast notes are called crotchets, they last for one beat.
- The slow notes are called **semibreves**, they last for four beats.
- Ask the children to sing along with the recording and to tap their fingers on the table in time with the coda notes.
- They should use alternate hands when doing the tapping – to simulate playing an instrument with alternate beaters.
- Ask the children what direction the notes are moving in – downwards in a stepping pattern.
- Using traditional stave notation, ask the children to work out the names of the notes:

  Five lines = **E**very **G**ood **B**oy **D**eserves **F**ootball
  Four spaces = **F A C E**.

- The notes required are: C C C C B B B B A A A A G G G G F F F F
  E E E E D D D D G G G G
    C   B   A   G   F   E   D   C

- At first it is best if the semibreve notes are hit only on the first beat and left to ring out for four beats.
- Later, it is possible to play the long semibreve notes using the tremolo technique (playing alternate beaters rapidly on one bar to provide a continuous sound).
- Once there has been sufficient practice of the coda, the children can sing the song and play the coda.

Variation

- Use the recording of the song as a backing track and play the coda when it comes. Ask the children to count the four beats in a bar as the song is playing to ensure they understand the difference between playing a one-beat crotchet and a four-beat semibreve.

Cross-curricular links

Maths – counting and directional language.

'**Do you like the taste?**'

Duet or Trio

Suitable for

KS1, KS2

Aims

- To develop the children's ability to keep their own rhythmic part going whilst playing along with others.
- To encourage several different rhythmic parts playing together.
- To increase the children's confidence in playing a rhythmic part.

Resources

- A variety of untuned percussion instruments
- A selection of rhythmic parts using initially the notes taa, tate and a one-beat rest (See p. 154 for some ideas for the rhythm parts.)

What to do

- Look at the rhythmic parts (see below) with the children and speak them through then clap them.
- Ask one child to choose a percussion instrument and one of the rhythmic parts.
- Ask them to play their part whilst the rest of the class listen and decide if it was played accurately or not.
- Choose a second child to pick another rhythmic part and an instrument to play it on.
- Again ask them to play their part whilst the rest of the class listen and decide if they played accurately or not.
- Now ask the two individuals to play their parts at the same time. It will be necessary for the leader of this activity to count them in: 1 2 3 4.
- Explain that these two children have played a **duet**.
- Now add a third child playing a different rhythmic part and this will form a **trio**.
- Ask the children to decide if they want to play as a duet or a trio and let them organise themselves into the appropriate groups and choose their instruments.

• Once they have practised in their own group, everyone can listen to each other.

Variations

• Instead of using classroom percussion instruments, body percussion could be used: clapping, stamping, tapping, rubbing hands together, clicking fingers, etc.
• Eventually, the duets and trios could be a mixture of percussion instruments and body percussion.

Cross-curricular links

PSHE – working as part of a team.
Language – observing rhythmic patterns in music and transferring them to words.
Maths – music with two or three participants using two, three or four beats – patterns of numbers.

Rhythmic Parts

Rhythm Rondo

Suitable for

KS1, KS2

Aims

- To introduce form into the rhythmic patterns the children produce.
- To encourage the children to be adventurous in their rhythmic compositions.
- To allow children the freedom to develop their own abilities in making rhythmic compositions.

Resources

- A selection of untuned percussion instruments
- A chart showing clearly the pattern that a **rondo** follows.

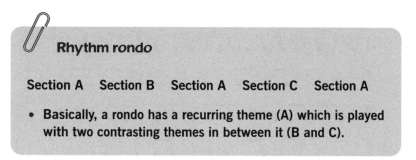

Rhythm rondo

Section A   Section B   Section A   Section C   Section A

- **Basically, a rondo has a recurring theme (A) which is played with two contrasting themes in between it (B and C).**

What to do

- Ask the children to make up a rhythm using the words 'rhythm' and 'rondo', e.g.:

  'Start the rhythm rondo here with theme A, we'll make it clear.'

- Ask the children to choose which percussion instrument(s) they would like to play this rhythm and practise getting the group playing together.

- Then ask a second group of children to make up a rhythm which contains the words 'theme B', e.g.:

  'Theme B is this tune's name, it's quite different – not the same.'

- Ask the children to choose contrasting instruments from theme A and let them practise getting their rhythmic pattern played together.
- Now play theme A, theme B, theme A.
- Next ask the remainder of the children to make up a rhythm which contains the words 'theme C', e.g.:

  'Theme C has a turn, it plays last but goes for the burn!'

- Ask the children to choose contrasting instruments from either themes A or B and let them practise getting their rhythmic pattern played together.
- Finally, play theme A, theme B, theme A, theme C, theme A. The class have performed their Rhythm Rondo!

Variation

- Use the percussion instruments in groups, i.e., wooden, shaking, scraping, and metal. Then decide which type of instrument plays in which theme of the rondo.

Cross-curricular links

Maths – following and continuing a pattern.
Language – following the rhythm of words and matching those rhythms to sounds.
Topic work – the words of the Rhythm Rondo could be about whatever topic is being studied.

'The Can Can'

Suitable for

KS1, KS2

Aims

- To enable the children to play several different rhythmic patterns along with a piece of classical music.
- To develop the children's abilities in keeping a rhythmic pattern going whilst other, different patterns are playing.
- To increase the children's understanding of **form** in music.

Resources

- A recording of 'The Can Can' by Offenbach (from an operetta called *Orpheus in the Underworld*)
- A CD player
- A chart showing clearly all the sections in 'The Can Can' music
- A selection of percussion instruments: tambourines, rhythm sticks, woodblocks, drums and triangles

What to do

- Let the children hear the recording of 'The Can Can'.
- As it is playing, point out the introduction.
- Point out section A with its long note followed by tate, tate rhythm.
- Point out section B with its tate, tate, tate, taa rhythm.
- Point out section C with its strong four beats followed by tate, tate, tate, taa.
- Also point out that section C is followed by the introduction music then section A again.
- The piece finishes off with the coda which has four strong beats followed by tate, tate, tate, taa then nine strong beats and the final flourish of da-da, da-da.
- Look at the chart of the music and point out the different sections of the music.
- Divide the class into groups with each group responsible for one of the sections.

- You will need five different groups.
- Ask each group to collect the instruments they require and allow them all some practice time.
- Go over each part carefully getting the group to play their part along with the recording.
- When all the groups are confident, play the recording and let them follow the chart to play their part in the correct place.

- A cymbal, snare drum and bass drum would be useful too

Variation

- Have the groups set out like an orchestra and either take the conductor's job yourself or ask a confident pupil to be the conductor.

Cross-curricular links

Maths – counting, noticing patterns and adapting to changes in patterns.
PSHE – working as part of a team, confidence building.

Introduction
Triangles

Section A
Tambourines
shake   shake

Section B
Rhythm
sticks

Section C
Drums
1 2 3 4   ← wood blocks

Introduction
Triangles

Section A
Tambourines
shake   shake

Coda
Bass drum
Cymbals
Snare drums
1 2 3 4   ← wood blocks

Bass drum
Cymbals
Snare drums
1 2 3 4 5 6 7 8 9 da-da da-da

'The Can Can' – Offenbach

Chapter 4
Listening

Introduction

'Music teaches beauty. Creating beauty is an act of compassion. When we make music, we are making the world a more beautiful place.' Nick Page

I have tried in this section to give as many different ideas as possible for introducing children to the wonderful world of listening to music. Hopefully the games and activities will allow the children the opportunity to listen with purpose and therefore enable them to gain an understanding of the importance of listening. All the activities encourage the children to become more aware of their environment and to constantly question the sounds they hear.

There is often movement with the listening and sometimes there is singing. The basic idea is that there needn't be a long piece of listening with no interruptions. I often help the children to focus on their listening by describing what is happening in the music as it is actually happening. In this day and age of CDs, it is incredibly easy to get to exactly the moment in a piece of music that you wish to talk about or demonstrate.

There are 12 advanced activities in this section:

- four musical instructions to help the children to move as a class.
- a little dance routine to a Victorian Music Hall song.
- an instrumental accompaniment to a sixties song.
- an introduction to the three-beat pattern of a waltz in which the children are encouraged to try to recognise a considerable number of melodies.
- providing the opportunity to recognise different sections in a piece of music.
- encouraging the children to illustrate a piece of music that tells a story.
- developing the memory skills of the children.
- a rhythmic accompaniment to a piece of ragtime music.
- an opportunity for a dramatic presentation about the music being listened to.
- a challenging fit of words to a piece of classical music.
- stretches the children's listening capabilities to try to recognise a note purely by its pitch.
- encourages the children to tell the story of the music they are listening to and to illustrate the story they have settled on.

I believe children have a much better chance of appreciating the music they are listening to if they are given some clear pointers as to what the music is trying to convey.

High or Low

Suitable for

KS1

Aims

- To develop the children's awareness of the difference between high and low sounds.
- To encourage the children to understand that high and low are different from loud and quiet.
- To encourage the children to listen to sounds in their environment and to sort those sounds into categories.

Resources

- A large selection of pictures containing items that make a high or low sound, e.g.: a whistle, baby crying, triangle, bass drum, a bird singing, a bass guitar, a bell ringing, a flute or piccolo, a ship's foghorn, a mouse, a siren blaring
- A board on which there are two sections entitled 'HIGH' and 'LOW'

What to do

- Show the pictures to the children and ask them to decide which category each picture/sound should go in to.
- This will probably require a fair amount of guidance from the leader as the children may confuse a loud volume with a high pitch and a low volume with a low pitch.
- It is beneficial to have a few real sound-making items in the classroom to demonstrate the low and high sounds.
- It is also helpful to relate the high and low sounds to the people on the solfa staircase (see pp. 8–9).
- Once all the pictures have been categorised, ask the children to come up with other suggestions and discuss which categories these suggestions should go in to.

Variations

- Each child could individually make their own 'Sounds Book' into which they put their own categories, e.g.: high, low, scraping, shaking, sad, happy.
- Each child or group of children could choose a category and use classroom instruments to make up a high, low, scraping, shaking, sad or happy piece of music.

Cross-curricular links

PSHE – discussion of emotions and how to express them.

Language – descriptive words and words for emotions.

Science – observing and recording experiments, investigating similarities and differences.

Maths – sorting into sets, noticing patterns, e.g., big = low, little = high.

'Teddy Bears' Picnic'

Suitable for

KS1

Aims

- To allow the children to move freely with a musical stimulus.
- To add appropriate actions and sound effects to a piece of music which tells a story.

Resources

- A recording of 'Teddy Bears' Picnic' by Henry Hall
- A CD player

What to do

- Ask the children to listen to the music right through and tell them that you will be asking questions about what happens in the song so that they have a reason for listening.
- After the first play through, ask questions such as:
  - What were the teddies going to do?
  - Where were they going?
  - Who was going to be there with them?
  - Did the music sound right for bears? Why?
- After discussing the song, listen to a short excerpt then stop the music and discuss with the children how they are going to dramatise the story.
- During the introduction it might be worth trying to move as teddy bears would in order to get to the woods.
- Decide how words like 'surprise' will be dramatised.
- Decide on a sequence that can be used for the phrase 'Today's the day the teddy bears have their picnic'.
- Go through the whole piece deciding what actions you want to do for each section of the music.
- Once the whole song has been covered, practise performing the actions whilst the music is playing.

- Once the children are confident at this, discuss the possibility of adding some percussion instruments for sound effects, e.g.:
  - drums for the bears walking
  - rhythm sticks for them playing in the woods
  - Indian bells for when the bears are getting tired, etc.

Variations

- Divide the class into groups and ask each group to be in charge of one part of the story. Get them to practise their own part and then insert it when it is appropriate during the song.

Cross·curricular links

Drama – telling a story through dramatic movement.
Language – listening and discussing a story.

Shake and Shoogle!

Suitable for

KS1

Aims

- To allow the children to respond physically to a sound.
- To encourage creativity in movement whilst listening.

Resources

- A maraca or any kind of shaker

What to do

- Ask the children to sit in a circle and hold their hands out in front of them with limp wrists, leaving their fingers dangling loosely.
- Tell them to close their eyes and let their hands respond to the sound they will hear.
- Play the maraca very slowly and gently, then with rapid movements, play a recognised rhythm, leave a few rests then repeat the rhythm.
- The children are free to move their hands in any way they think is appropriate.
- Once this has been done, ask the children about what was making them move and they will reply 'the shaker'.
- Explain that the sound they heard had an effect on their body and the movements they made depended on how the sound was produced.
- Next ask the children to stand in their circle and to move their whole body when they hear the shaker (it is probably best if their feet stay stuck to the floor!).
- Discuss with the children which parts of the body can shake – legs, elbows, eyebrows, hair, hands, lips, etc.

Variations

- Choose a different instrument and therefore a different way of moving, e.g.:
  - guiro = creeping
  - drum = thumping
  - triangle = moving delicately as if walking on glass.

Cross-curricular links

Drama – expressive movement in response to music.
PE – movement, coordination.

Fire-Bell Polka

Suitable for

KS1

Aims

- To help children to follow a piece of music using a movement routine.
- To encourage recognition of a piece of music by breaking it down into sections.
- To encourage movement in time with a beat and melody.

Resources

- A recording of 'The Anvil Polka', by Josef Strauss
- A CD player
- A copy of the movement routine for the leader

What to do

- Explain to the children that they are going to do a dance about being a fire-fighter.
- Let the children listen to the music and ask them to tell you every time they hear the fire bell.
- Discuss the routine of the fire-fighters when the fire bell rings in the fire station.
- Try the movement for the introduction.
- Make a bell-ringing movement above your head then count to five and repeat this three times.
- The words that go along with section A fit to the melody for that section.
- The children should sing the words as they do the actions.
- The same is the case with section B and the children act out the words as the music is playing.
- Section A is then played twice followed by section C.
- In section C, the children are acting out holding the very heavy water hose and spraying the water on the fire.
- In section D, the words are spoken rather than sung and are acted out in time to the music.

- The children go into the building, lift the casualty over their shoulder, reverse out of the building and lay the casualty on the ground.
- They repeat this process four times.
- After a reprise of sections A, B and A there is the coda.
- In the coda, the children stand to attention, salute, stand to attention, salute, run on the spot then stand absolutely still to attention.
- The dance is quite strenuous and the children are likely to be out of breath by the end of it!

Variation

- It is possible to only move at the section A part of the music and simply listen to the other tunes.

Cross-curricular links

PE – aerobic exercise.

Topic work – fits with a topic of people who help us or safety.

Introduction: ♩ 1 2 3 4 5 ♩ 1 2 3 4 5 ♩ 1 2 3 4 5 🔔

A ♫ ♫ 1 2 3 4 ♫ ♫ 1 2 3 4 ⎫
⎬ × 4
Put your hat on, slide down Put your hat on, slide down ⎭
the pole.　　　　　　　　the pole.

B 1 2 3 4 ♫♫ ♫ ♫ ♫ ♩ 𝄾 ⎫
⎬ × 3
run _ _ _ _ climb in the engine, sit down, off we go. ⎭

1 2 3 4 5 🔔 1 2 3 4 5 🔔 ♪ ♩🔔♪ ♩🔔♪ ♩🔔♪ ♫ ♫ ♫ ♩
Driving to the fire _

A × 2

C 1 2 3 4 ♫♫♫ ♫ ♫ ♫♫♫ ♫ ♫ ♫♫♫ ♩♩ ⎫
⎬ × 4
Out of the　hold the　hose　and scoosh　the　water　here ⎭
fire engine,

D 1 2 3 4　5 6 7 8 ‖ 1 2 3 4　5 6 7 8 ⎫
⎬ × 4
Into the building, save somebody,　reverse back out, lay them down ⎭

♪ ♩ ♪ ♩ ♪ 1 2 3 4 5 🔔

A × 2

B 1 2 3 4 ♫♫ ♫ ♫ ♫ ♩ 𝄾
run _ _ _ _ climb in the engine, sit down, off we go.

1 2 3 4 5 🔔 1 2 3 4 5 🔔 ♪ ♩🔔♪ ♩🔔♪ ♩🔔♪ ♫ ♫ ♫ ♩

A × 2 drum ♩ drum ♩ 1 2 3 4 5
stand, salute, stand, salute,　run on　stand still
the spot,

Fire-Bell Polka

Pat, Pat, Patterns

Suitable for

KS1, KS2

Aims

- To hear and keep a beat.
- To sustain variations in patterns whilst moving to music.

Resources

- CD player
- CD of music with a strong beat: marching band music, number from a musical, e.g., 'We're All in this Together' from *High School Musical*

What to do

- Listen to the piece of music and tap the beat on your hand.
- Listen again and count

  1   2   3   4 (for younger classes) or
  1   2   3   4   5   6   7   8 (for older classes).

- Listen again and pat both hands on knees for counts 1 2 then continue counting, e.g.:

  pat, pat 3   4   5   6   7   8.

- Ask the children for suggestions as to an action for beats 3 and 4, e.g.:

  pat, pat, clap, clap 5   6   7   8.

- Listen again and do the pattern so far.
- Ask the children for suggestions as to an action for beats 5 and 6, e.g.:

  pat, pat, clap, clap, touch alternate elbows.

- Listen again and do the pattern so far.
- Ask the children for suggestions as to an action for beats 7 and 8, e.g., pat alternate cheeks.

- Listen again and do the whole pattern:

pat	pat	clap	clap	elbow	elbow	cheek	cheek
1	2	3	4	5	6	7	8

Variations

- Once the pattern is established, add a second pattern, but make sure to always have pat, pat on beats 1 and 2 – this gives thinking time for changing between pattern one and pattern two.
- Once pattern one and pattern two are established, add pattern three.

> **Giving the patterns names helps to remind the class which one is coming up, e.g.:**
>
> **Pattern one – elbow, cheeks pattern**
> **Pattern two – click and head pattern.**

Cross-curricular links

Science – body parts.
Topic work – choose music appropriate to the topic, e.g.:
- – Romans: 'Hold High the Eagle'
- – Africa: 'Jambo Bwana'.

Maths – counting and patterns, sequencing.

Hide and Seek Sounds

Suitable for

KS1, KS2

Aims

- To encourage discrimination in listening.
- To practise identification of sounds.
- To encourage experimentation in making sounds.

Resources

- A screen for hiding behind
- A collection of instruments and anything that makes a sound

What to do

- At first the teacher – but later a child – chooses a sound maker and makes the sound behind the screen.
- The children have to guess what is making the sound.
- With percussion instruments, there are many ways of making a sound, e.g.: tambourine: shake, tap, scrape fingers on the skin, tap fingernails on the metal bits.
- With a selection of sound makers, it might be an idea to show the selection to the children before playing the game.

Variations

- Choose one instrument, e.g., tambourine, and have a competition to see how many different ways it can be played. The person who guesses how the sound is being produced then goes behind the screen and tries a different way of making a sound.
- Have more than one sound being produced, e.g., tambourine and maraca. It's perhaps helpful to show the selection of sound makers you're choosing from. There is still plenty of scope for being ingenious in the way you play!

Cross-curricular links

Language – descriptive language.
Science – how sound is produced.
PSHE – problem solving together.

Fantastic Four

Suitable for

KS1, KS2

Aims

- To recognise the sound of the four families of orchestral instruments – **brass**, **strings**, **woodwind**, **percussion**.
- To be aware of the standard orchestral instruments in each family:
  Brass – tuba, trombone, trumpet, French horn
  Strings – harp, double bass, cello, viola, violin
  Woodwind – bassoon, clarinet, flute, oboe
  Percussion – drums, cymbals, tambourine, glockenspiel, xylophone, sleigh bells (basically anything you hit!)

> **Some orchestras consider the harp as a member of the string section and others have it in the percussion section.**

Resources

- CD player
- Pictures of orchestral instruments
- CDs of a variety of music featuring the four different families of instruments: brass band, string orchestra, wind band, percussion band and also some solo instrumental music

What to do

- Play the class a piece of music for each family of the orchestra.
- If possible, show appropriate pictures whilst the music is playing.
- Suitable excerpts could be: brass band playing hymns, wind band playing marches, string orchestra playing some Mozart, Evelyn Glennie playing xylophone/glockenspiel.

- Have a selection of music available and as it is playing, ask the children to listen and try to work out which family of instruments is playing.
- In the case of solo instruments, the children should try to identify the instrument first and then give its family name.

Variations

- Ask the children to bring in a piece of instrumental music and get the class to recognise the instrument and/or family.
- Use TV themes/adverts, e.g.
  - *Coronation Street* – trumpet
  - *South Bank Show* – cello.

Cross-curricular links

Science – the larger the instrument, the lower the sound. The smaller the instrument, the higher the sound.
Language – vocabulary used in describing the names and families of instruments.

Hup 2, 3, 4

Suitable for

KS1, KS2

Aims

- To hear and feel the pulse and beat of a piece of music.
- To be able to work out an appropriate way of moving to music.
- Playing untuned percussion instruments.

Resources

- CD player
- CD of marching music – any march by Sousa or a military band playing a march
- A selection of untuned percussion instruments: rhythm sticks/claves, tambourines, maracas, drums, woodblocks

What to do

- Play the recording and ask the children to sit and tap the beat of the music with one finger on their palm.
- In a march the beat is most commonly counted 1 2 3 4 or Hup 2 3 4.
- Next, ask the children to march on the spot saying Hup 2 3 4.
- Ask the children to march around the room to the music and clap on 'Hup' whilst continuing to march on 2 3 4.
- Give a drum to a child who is visibly managing to feel the 'Hup' clearly, and ask them to become the marching band leader.
- Gradually add more instruments with clear instructions for how they should be played, e.g.: a maraca in each hand playing alternate sides on <u>1</u> 2 <u>3</u> 4.
- Rhythm sticks tapped above the head only on 2 3 4 and brought down to the sides on 'Hup'.
- Tambourine held high on 'Hup' and shaken downwards on 2 3 4. Rest for the next Hup 2 3 4 then repeat with the tambourine on the other side.
- Woodblock being hit only on 'Hup' and silent for 2 3 4.

Variations

- As many different instruments as you like.
- You could decide on certain instruments playing alone in certain sections of the music.
- You could make up a marching routine based on the different instrument sections with the whole band marching and playing together at some parts.

Cross·curricular links

PSHE – movement and cooperation, teambuilding.

Maths – counting and patterns, sequencing.

Topic work – choose music appropriate to the topic being studied.

Sounds Around

Suitable for

KS1, KS2

Aims

- To develop listening skills.
- To develop the ability to identify sounds.
- To associate sounds with pictures.

Resources

- CD player
- Recording of a variety of everyday sounds which match prepared pictures, e.g.: alarm clock, striking match, breaking glass, nose blowing, gurgling water, teaspoon stirring a cup, audience clapping
- A screen for hiding objects behind
- Several objects for dropping, e.g. bunch of keys, bouncy ball, pen, book

What to do

- Ask the class to listen and then list sounds they can hear whilst sitting in the room.
- As each sound is named, stop until everyone can identify that sound.
- Next, have someone hold up two objects, e.g.: keys and a book, then drop one of them behind the screen.
- Everyone should try to identify which one was dropped by the sound it made.
- Increase the number of items shown.
- Study the pictures of various sounds.
- Listen to recordings of those sounds and try to match the pictures with the sounds.

Variation

- A game of sound lotto can be played with cards which have six or eight sound pictures and a recording of several sounds. As each sound is identified, the picture is covered. The winner is the first to cover all their pictures.

Cross-curricular links

Language – descriptions of sounds.

Science – how sounds are produced and using the senses.

'Thunder and Lightning Polka'

Suitable for

KS1 and KS2

Aims

- To help children to follow a piece of music using a movement routine.
- To encourage recognition of a piece of music by breaking it down into sections.
- To encourage movement in time with a beat and melody.

Resources

- A recording of the 'Thunder and Lightning Polka', by Johann Strauss II
- A CD player
- A copy of the movement routine for the leader

What to do

- Let the children simply listen to the music and ask them to let you know when they hear cymbals or drums.
- Explain that they are going to learn a little dance for each section of the polka and there will be four sections in all named A, B, C and D.
- At the end of the polka there is a coda which is a finishing off piece of music.
- Start by teaching the dance to tune A:
  - The 'step forward' part fits to the first half of the tune and the clapping is to the rhythm that is being played in the second half of the tune.
- This pattern is repeated several times.
- Between each tune there is a little introduction.
- Once the children are confident at the dance for tune A, play the piece right through and help them to perform the dance for tune A on the two occasions that they hear the tune A melody.
- Next teach the dance for tune B:
  - The 'step close' covers the first half of the tune and the second half of the tune is for the feet-touching routine.

- Play the piece through and ask the children in parts A and B to do their movement as appropriate.
- Teach the dance for tune C:
  - The walking around for four is easy, but the down, up part is extremely strenuous and may result in sore legs the next day!
- The dance for tune D is the easiest dance. Again, the movements fit to the rhythm of the tune.
- Finally, perform the whole polka.

Variation

- Try to make up your own movements for the coda that are appropriate for a big finish.

Cross-curricular links

PE – aerobic exercise.
Topic work – fits with a topic of weather.

TUNE A

Step forward, step forward ♪. ♩ ♪. ♩ ♩ (clap)

Step backwards, step backwards ♪. ♩ ♪. ♩ ♩ (clap)

TUNE B

To the right: step close, step close, touch left ankle with right foot.
touch right ankle with left foot.

To the left: step close, step close, touch right ankle with left foot.
touch left ankle with right foot.

TUNE C

Walk round in a circle for the count of four
down, up, down, up, down, up

TUNE D

Both hands: head, shoulders ♪. ♩ ♩ (pat your knees)

TUNE C
TUNE A
TUNE B
Coda

'Thunder and Lightning Polka'

Classroom Rumble

Suitable for

KS1, KS2

Aims

- To develop the children's ability to listen to each other's compositions.
- To encourage individual contributions to a class composition.
- To encourage careful listening whilst playing.

Resources

- A classroom that the children can explore for sounds
- A piece of equipment capable of recording

What to do

- Ask the children to sit at their desks in the classroom and listen carefully.
- What sounds can they hear from within their classroom?
- Next, ask the children to look carefully and find something from within the classroom that they can make a sound with, e.g., two pencils clicking, a door handle squeaking, a pencil rattling over a radiator, etc.
- Ask each child individually to say what their sound is.
- Either ask each child to play their sound – potentially ending up with 30 different sounds or put the class into groups of sounds with maybe six different groups.
- Each group or individual describes how their sound is being produced and decides if it is similar or different to any of the other sounds, e.g. in the way it is produced.
- Using the sounds, make up a 'Chance Composition' by giving each group or individual a number and that is the order the composition is played in.
- Make sure the children realise that they will need to have very clear beginnings and endings to their playing part so that the composition can flow.

Variation

- Divide the class into groups of five or six and ask each group to produce a Chance Composition using classroom sounds.

Cross-curricular links

Science – how sound is produced, what makes a loud/quiet sound.
Language – descriptive language for how the sound is produced and comparison with other sounds.
PSHE – team work and confidence building.

'Pennsylvania 6-5000'

Suitable for

KS2

Aims

- To introduce the children to music from the 1940s and Glenn Miller in particular.
- To develop the children's skills in playing several untuned percussion instruments.
- To develop the children's skills in playing tuned percussion and reading traditional notation.
- To encourage children to feel the beat of a piece of music.

Resources

- A white or black board on which to write the rhythmic parts, order of sections and tuned percussion parts
- A recording of 'Pennsylvania 6–5000' by the Glenn Miller Band
- A CD player
- Tuned and untuned percussion instruments
- Two matching beaters for each tuned percussion instrument

What to do

- Let the children hear the recording of 'Pennsylvania 6–5000'.
- Explain that the piece of music is written with the phone number of a hotel as its inspiration.
- Ask the children to look at the way the sections are played during the piece – what do they notice?
- Section A is played a lot more than any other section so start by teaching a small group of children the notes they require for playing section A: G# played six times, C played six times and C# played six times.
- The timing for these notes is 1 2 3 4 slow, slow.
- Once the children are confident at playing these notes they could try playing along with the recording.
- Divide the rest of the class into groups of tambourines, rhythm sticks and maracas.

• The untuned percussion parts are basically just counting parts, so each group must check to see if they play their part once, twice or three times.
• If wished, an individual could play the snare drum part.
• Once everyone is confident with their part, try playing the recording with everyone joining with it, keeping their timing very clear.

Variation

• To make things simpler, the parts need not all be used at the same time.

Cross-curricular links

History – 1940s music, Glenn Miller and the Big Band scene.
Maths – counting and keeping to a pattern.

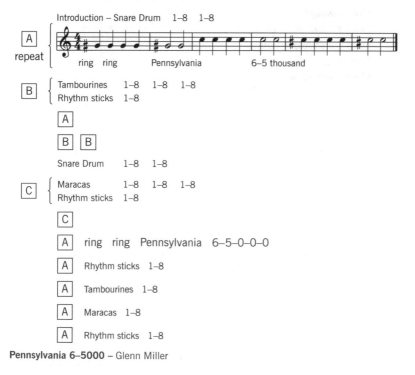

Pennsylvania 6–5000 – Glenn Miller

'The Syncopated Clock'

Suitable for

KS1, KS2

Aims

- To introduce the children to a piece of music that paints a picture.
- To develop the children's knowledge and understanding of an orchestra.
- To encourage the children to understand how a piece of music is constructed.

Resources

- A recording of 'The Syncopated Clock' by Leroy Anderson
- A CD player
- A copy of the chart to go with the following music:

> **Flute – woodblock (whizz)**
> *Piano – clarinet (woodblock)*
> **Flute – woodblock (whizz)**
> *Piano – clarinet (woodblock)*
> **Flute – woodblock**

What to do

- Before listening to the music, discuss clocks with the children and particularly the tick-tock sound that they make.
- Discuss all the different sounds associated with clocks, e.g. chimes, ticking, ringing, donging, etc.
- Explain the chart before listening to the music.
- There are basically two different sections in the music:

  The flute (a woodwind instrument) is played out at the side of the body and has a high breathy sound. With the flute part of the music you also hear a woodblock and a peculiar whizz sound. This is indicated in the chart by the bold text.

  The piano (a percussion instrument because of the hammers that hit the strings inside the piano) section also uses another woodwind instrument – the clarinet. The clarinet has a deeper, mellower sound than the flute. During the piano section a woodblock is heard. This is indicated in the chart by the italicised text.

• Play the music to the children and ask them to indicate when each section and instrument is playing.

Variation

• Having listened to the music and discussed the ticking sounds a clock makes, ask the children to use classroom percussion instruments to play along with the recording to add some ticking sounds to the music.

Cross-curricular links

Science – how things work.
Language – descriptive language for the music, instruments and the clock workings.
Maths – noticing patterns and sequences.

Instrumental Sets

Suitable for

KS1, KS2

Aims

- To increase the children's knowledge of orchestral instruments and how they are played.
- To encourage the children to think about how sound is produced.

Resources

- A board on which there are three columns with the headings:

  Strings   Blowing   Hitting

- A large selection of recordings of solo orchestral instruments
- A large selection of pictures of orchestral instruments

What to do

- Let the children hear a recording of an orchestral instrument and if possible have the appropriate picture available as well.
- Ask the children to decide which category each instrument should go in to.
- With some instruments this may cause a bit of discussion as, for instance, the harp is placed in the string section in some orchestras and the percussion section in others.
- Perhaps some instruments will need to appear in more than one column.
- Generally, the definition of a percussion instrument is 'something that is hit or struck'.

Variation

- Once the children have tried this exercise with orchestral instruments they could go on to categorise the classroom percussion instruments using different headings, e.g.:

  Scraping   Shaking   Hitting

Cross-curricular links

Science – observing and recording experiments, investigating similarities and differences.

Language – descriptive words, debate as to which column an instrument should be in.

Maths – sorting into sets, noticing patterns.

Loud or Quiet

Suitable for

KS1, KS2

Aims

- To enable the children to understand the difference between loud and quiet.
- To encourage the children to investigate the sounds around them, in their environment.
- To encourage the children to connect a symbol with either loud or quiet.

Resources

- A selection of percussion instruments

What to do

- Ask the children to suggest some quiet sounds they may hear every day, e.g.:
  a cat purring
  a pin dropping
  leaves rustling
  the rubbing of a hand over a surface, etc.
- Next ask the children to suggest some loud sounds they may hear every day, e.g.:
  a shout
  a door banging
  a plate dropping and smashing
  a car engine revving, etc.
- Make two lists headed **Loud** and **Quiet** and put the various sounds discussed under one of the headings.
- Next ask the children if they can produce either quiet or loud sounds with their voices or bodies, e.g. ssh, rubbing fingers together, stamping feet, screaming, etc.
- Add their suggestions to the lists headed **Loud** and **Quiet**.
- Now divide the class into groups of five or six children.
- Ask each group to choose three sounds from each list and make a visual representation of each sound.

- Once the groups have done this, ask them to organise these symbols into a piece that they can perform.
- They may have to produce more than one of some of the symbols if they wish to repeat a sound in their composition.
- Explain that each group can use percussion instruments and their voices and bodies to produce their piece.
- Ask each group to perform their Loud and Quiet piece to the other children.

Variations

- Instead of using everyday sounds, the children could suggest words that are either quiet or loud, e.g. whisper, shout, mumble, scream, bellow, sob, etc.
- Once they have made a list of words, they could produce either a Quiet poem or a Loud poem using only words from their lists.

Cross-curricular links

Language – exploration of words, meanings and usage.
Science – observing and recording experiments, investigating similarities and differences.
Maths – sorting into sets, noticing patterns.

How Many Sounds?

Suitable for

KS1, KS2

Aims

- To give practice at playing and improvising on percussion instruments.
- To develop listening skills.

Resources

- A selection of percussion instruments – tuned and untuned
- Two matching beaters for any tuned percussion instrument

What to do

- Have the children all sit in a circle with one child blindfolded in the middle.
- The instruments are all around the circle, perhaps even allocated one to each child.
- The class chant:

   How many sounds can you hear today?
   How many sounds and what did we play?

- One child from around the circle then plays a random number of notes on their instrument.
- The child who is blindfolded then has to say how many notes were played and on which instrument.
- Everyone is required to listen as they can all decide if the answer given is correct or not.
- Once the blindfolded child has guessed, the child who played gets to sit in the middle and do the guessing for the next time.

Variations

- The person playing the notes can make a little rhythm or melody up as they go, giving them a chance to try some improvisation.
- The leader could indicate that only certain rhythms are to be played, e.g. taa and tate; then the child who is guessing has to specify which rhythms were played as well as what instrument was used.

Cross-curricular links

Language – knowing the names of all the percussion instruments.
PSHE – developing listening skills in a group setting.
Maths – counting.

Good Sound/Bad Sound

Suitable for

KS1, KS2

Aims

- To encourage the children to be aware of sounds all around them.
- To allow the children to explore the sounds all around them.
- To give the children an opportunity to share their opinions about various sounds.

Resources

- Two tables or areas with labels '**Good**' and '**Bad**'

What to do

- The leader of this activity brings in two objects that make a sound.
- One of the objects must make a sound that the leader likes, e.g., a hot water bottle with water in it.
- The other object must make a sound that the leader does not like, e.g., chalk screeching on a blackboard.
- As the leader puts each object on to the table they must say what it is they like or dislike about the sound and allow the class to agree or disagree and give their opinions too.
- Ask the children to bring in objects of their own and when they place them on the table they must tell the class what it is they like or dislike about the sounds.

Variation

- Have a 'Box of Sounds' and let an individual child divide the sounds between the two tables. They must be able to say why any object is put on one of the tables.

Cross-curricular links

Language – being able to give reasons for an action, debating skills.
PSHE – having an opinion about something and being able to share that opinion.

Stand Up/Sit Down

Suitable for

KS1, KS2

Aims

- To develop the children's understanding and awareness of pitch.
- To encourage careful listening for changes in pitch.

Resources

- A copy of the solfa staircase (see pp. 7, 8, 9) with only so and purple doe in place on the staircase
- A tuned instrument, e.g.: piano, glockenspiel, violin, etc. on which the two notes G and C (higher than the G) are to be played

What to do

- Have the children all sitting on chairs – in a circle if desired but it is not essential.
- Practise playing the notes G then C (so, doe) and singing 'Stand up' when you play them.
- Practise playing the notes the other way round: C then G (doe, so) and singing 'Sit down' when you play them.
- At each playing, the children do whichever action is requested.
- Once the children are confident at this, play the notes but don't say the action and see how many children manage to connect the rising notes with 'Stand up' and the falling notes with 'Sit down'.
- Discuss with the children what it is that they are actually doing, i.e., when the sound goes up, they stand up and when the sound goes down, they sit down.
- Practise this several times, mixing up the played instructions and allowing time for everyone to hear the difference in the notes.

Variation

- Once the children are confident at this game, add a third instruction playing the note G followed by the C that is lower than it (so, red doe). For this instruction, the children have to 'Lie down'. Practise in the same way as you did with the first two instructions until the class can respond to three musical instructions without any need for words being used.

Cross-curricular links

PE – movement and coordination.
Language – instructions and how to follow them.

Advanced

Up and Down or Left and Right

Suitable for

KS1, KS2

Aims

- To develop listening skills to a level where it is possible to take musical instructions for movements.
- To encourage careful listening.
- To reinforce the ascending, descending, high and low concepts.

Resources

- A tuned percussion instrument and two matching beaters
- A large space to allow for free movement
- Four A4 size instruction cards containing the music for the four instructions

What to do

- Explain to the children that they are going to be told four different instructions they will need to follow.
- The directions they will need to move in are dictated by the notes being played on the percussion instrument.
- Decide where the centre of the room is and which way is left, right, up and down from there.
- Start with Card 1 which contains a stave with the notes C D E F G ascending.
- Discuss with the children that these notes move from the left to the right on the glockenspiel/xylophone.
- When they hear these notes they need to move five paces to their right.
- Play the notes on Card 1 a few times and make sure the children can hear the ascending notes.
- Move on to Card 2 which contains a stave with the notes G F E D C descending.
- Discuss with the children that these notes move from the right to the left on the glockenspiel/xylophone.

- When they hear these notes they need to move five paces to their left.
- Practise with only the two instructions available and at first check with the class after you have played the notes to ensure they have correctly understood the direction of the notes and therefore the direction they need to move in.
- Once the children are confident with these two cards, introduce Card 3 which contains the notes low C E G and high C.
- These notes are jumping upwards so the children need to take four steps towards the top of the room when they hear these notes.
- Practise using three instructions, e.g., move five steps to the right, move five steps to the left or move four steps towards the top of the room.
- Once the children are confident with this, introduce Card 4 which contains a stave with the notes high C G E and low C.
- These notes are jumping downwards so the children need to take four steps towards the bottom of the room when they hear these notes.
- Practise first with only Cards 3 and 4 to help the children recognise the notes either jumping up or down and only when they are very confident with this, introduce all four cards.
- Very careful listening will be required to execute all four instructions correctly.
- At first, it may be necessary to pause after each set of notes and check that everyone has managed to decipher the instruction.
- Eventually, with lots of practice, it is possible to give the instruction musically and wait for the children to move in the correct direction.

Variations

- Have the majority of the class listening and only one or two 'movers'. Those listening have to say whether or not the 'mover' moved correctly or not.
- Have a child play the instructions and have another child interpret the instructions for the rest of the class. Obviously, the rest of the class have to check they are being given the correct interpretation.

Cross-curricular links

Maths – directional skills.

Language – directional language.

PSHE – working as part of a team and relying on others.

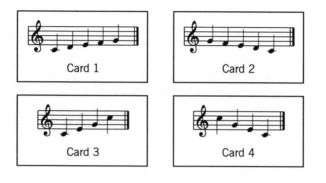

'Alexander's Ragtime Band'

Suitable for

KS1, KS2

Aims

- To help children to follow a piece of music using a movement routine.
- To encourage movement in time with a beat and melody.

Resources

- A recording of the song 'Alexander's Ragtime Band', by Irving Berlin
- A CD player
- A copy of the movement routine for the leader

What to do

- Give a bit of background about ragtime – what kind of music ragtime is, the history of ragtime through slavery and leading into blues and jazz.
- Let the children hear the song.
- Explain that this song would have been popular in the Victorian music hall.
- The class are going to learn a dance routine to go with the song and it is divided into only two sections with a short interlude between them.
- Teach the movements for section A:
  - 'Duster hands' means making a movement as if you were dusting around in a circle. The dusting should be done with an eager look on the face.
  - The marching is on the spot with knees moving upwards and arms swinging.
  - 'Elbows and knees travelling' means both elbows and knees moving simultaneously inwards and outwards whilst travelling along to the left or right.
- Play the music and ask the children to do the movements for section A each time they hear the appropriate words.

- Teach the movements for section B:
  - 'Crossover knees' means putting you hands on your knees and crossing them over and back for eight beats.
  - 'Crossover shoulders' is the same but on the shoulders.
  - The step forward and backwards and clap is self-explanatory.
  - 'Shoulder cross, bottom, bottom' means put left hand on right shoulder, then right hand on left shoulder, then left hand on left bottom cheek and right hand on right bottom cheek.
- Now play the music and put in both section A and section B.
- Teach the movements for the interlude:
  - The children mime playing a trumpet first of all to their left and they play it up in the air and then down towards the floor.
  - They then move the trumpet to their right and do the same.
- Teach the coda movements:
  - Walk round in a circle for four beats then use both hands to touch your head, your shoulders, clap then stretch arms out to finish.

Variation

- Only move in one section and perhaps add untuned percussion instruments to be part of 'Alexander's Ragtime Band'.

Cross-curricular links

PE – aerobic exercise.

Topic work – fits with a topic about Victorians.

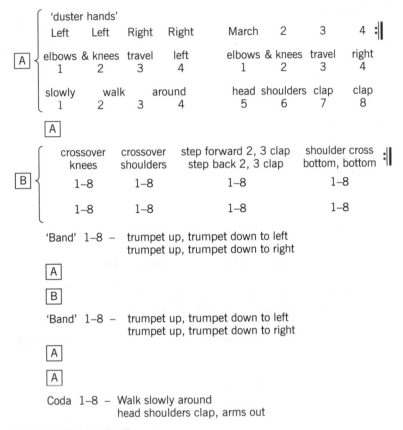

A
- 'duster hands'
  Left   Left   Right   Right   March   2   3   4 :‖
- elbows & knees   travel   left   elbows & knees   travel   right
    1   2   3   4   1   2   3   4
- slowly   walk   around   head shoulders clap   clap
    1   2   3   4   5   6   7   8

A

B
- crossover   crossover   step forward 2, 3 clap   shoulder cross :‖
  knees   shoulders   step back 2, 3 clap   bottom, bottom
    1–8   1–8   1–8   1–8
-   1–8   1–8   1–8   1–8

'Band' 1–8 – trumpet up, trumpet down to left
                trumpet up, trumpet down to right

A

B

'Band' 1–8 – trumpet up, trumpet down to left
                trumpet up, trumpet down to right

A

A

Coda 1–8 – Walk slowly around
               head shoulders clap, arms out

'Alexander's Ragtime Band'

'Zabadak'

Suitable for

KS2

Aims

- To introduce the children to music from the 1960s.
- To develop the children's skills in playing several rhythmic parts together.
- To develop the children's skills in playing tuned percussion and reading traditional notation.

Resources

- A white or black board on which to write the rhythmic and tuned percussion parts
- A recording of 'Zabadak' by Dave, Dee, Dozy, Beaky, Mick and Tich
- A CD player
- Tuned and untuned percussion instruments
- Two matching beaters for each tuned instrument

What to do

- Let the children hear the recording of 'Zabadak'.
- Ask the children to try singing the chorus which contains made-up words.
- Starting with the drum part, teach the untuned percussion parts to a small group of children.
- The two different notes in the drum part indicate which hands to use for playing the drum.
- The guiro part is mostly rests so it is important for the children to count carefully and to realise that they are playing only on beat two of a four-beat bar.
- The maraca part is fairly straightforward and could easily have words to help the children play it, e.g., shake, shake, zabadak.
- The tuned percussion part is the melody of the verses and has a sequence of notes which are fairly slow as they are two-beat notes.

The notes used are:

D E F# G, E F# G A , F# G A B D D
D E F# G, E F# G A, F# G A B B B

- Once each group has practised their part and can play it confidently, try putting them all together along with the recorded track.

Variation

- Either the rhythmic or tuned parts can be played alone with the children singing the chorus of the piece. A different untuned percussion instrument could be played for each of the made-up words.

Cross-curricular links

History – 1960s music and culture, a famous group from the 1960s.
Language – making up words, the rhythm of words.
PSHE – working in groups, confidence building.

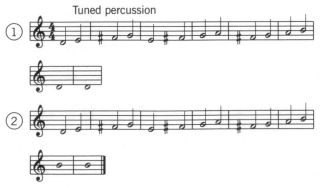

Percussion parts for 'Zabadak'

Oom Pah Pah

Suitable for

KS1, KS2

Aims

- To increase the children's knowledge of the waltz form in music.
- To develop the children's bank of listening material.
- To encourage and develop the use of three beats in a bar.

Resources

- A recording of the 'Blue Danube Waltz' by Johann Strauss the Younger
- A CD player

What to do

- Explain that the waltz is a dance form and if possible give a demonstration of how to dance a waltz.
- In a waltz there are always three beats in a bar.
- Play the first part of the recording of the 'Blue Danube' waltz and ask the children to count 1 2 3 as the music is playing.
- Explain that Johann Strauss was famous for composing numerous waltzes and the 'Blue Danube' is actually a set of five waltzes each with two tunes.
- The river called the Danube is a very long river that flows through several countries in Europe.
- The first tune in the piece is the tune that most people recognise as the 'Blue Danube' tune.
- The second tune is made up of lots of short notes with longer notes at the end.
- The third tune has some repeated notes at the beginning followed by a leap up to a very high note.
- The fourth tune has a flowing tune to begin with followed by high, short notes.
- The fifth tune starts off with a jumpy tune and then has low, repeated notes.
- The sixth tune has very fast, stepping notes followed by short, jerky notes later.

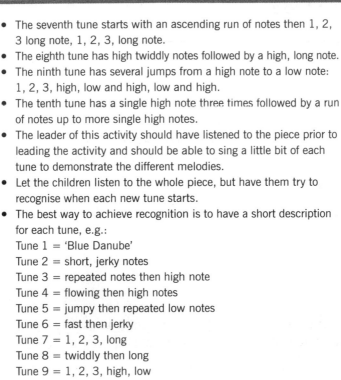

- The seventh tune starts with an ascending run of notes then 1, 2, 3 long note, 1, 2, 3, long note.
- The eighth tune has high twiddly notes followed by a high, long note.
- The ninth tune has several jumps from a high note to a low note: 1, 2, 3, high, low and high, low and high.
- The tenth tune has a single high note three times followed by a run of notes up to more single high notes.
- The leader of this activity should have listened to the piece prior to leading the activity and should be able to sing a little bit of each tune to demonstrate the different melodies.
- Let the children listen to the whole piece, but have them try to recognise when each new tune starts.
- The best way to achieve recognition is to have a short description for each tune, e.g.:
  Tune 1 = 'Blue Danube'
  Tune 2 = short, jerky notes
  Tune 3 = repeated notes then high note
  Tune 4 = flowing then high notes
  Tune 5 = jumpy then repeated low notes
  Tune 6 = fast then jerky
  Tune 7 = 1, 2, 3, long
  Tune 8 = twiddly then long
  Tune 9 = 1, 2, 3, high, low
  Tune 10 = three high notes then runs.

Variations

- After listening to the piece, ask the children to produce their own waltz using the rhythm 'Oom, pah, pah' as the basis for their composition.
- Ask them to use two different untuned percussion instruments – one for the 'Oom' and the other for the 'pah, pah'.
- Once they have established this rhythm, they could either sing a melody or try to **compose** one on a tuned percussion instrument.

Cross-curricular links

Topic work – would fit well with a topic of Europe or water.
Language – description of each tune.
Maths – noticing patterns and counting beats.

Sleigh Ride

Suitable for

KS1, KS2

Aims

- To introduce the children to a piece of classical music.
- To develop the children's knowledge of orchestral instruments.
- To develop the children's knowledge of how a piece of music is constructed.

Resources

- A recording of 'Troika' from the suite of music for the film *Lieutenant Kije* by the composer Prokofiev
- A CD player
- A chart depicting the music in sections which are colour-coded

> **The following chart will help the children as they listen and identify certain features in the music.**

Introduction
SLEIGH BELL TUNE
Pizzicato strings
Brass instruments
SLEIGH BELL TUNE
Pizzicato strings
Bassoon
SLEIGH BELL TUNE
Pizzicato strings
Brass instruments
Bassoon
SLEIGH BELL TUNE
Coda

What to do

- Give the children a little background information about the piece of music they are going to listen to:
  - Prokofiev – a Russian composer – wrote this music for a sleigh ride as part of a bigger group of music which was to be used to illustrate a film about the invented adventures of an imaginary soldier called Lieutenant Kije.
  - 'The Troika' describes a sleigh ride that Lieutenant Kije takes across the Russian plain.
- Before listening to the music, remind the children what an introduction and a coda are:
  - An introduction is a short piece to set the scene of the music and a coda is a finishing off piece of music.
- The blue sleigh bell tune is a melody that keeps returning and has sleigh bell accompaniment.
- The red pizzicato strings section highlights the string instruments (violin, viola, cello and double bass) plucking their strings instead of using the bow.
- The green section is where the brass instruments feature (trumpet, trombone, French horn and tuba).
- The orange bassoon section features the largest instrument in the woodwind section – the bassoon.
- Once all these sections have been discussed and pictures of the various instruments have been studied, the children can use the chart to follow what is happening in the music.

Variation

- Once the children have heard the music a few times and followed the chart, they can try to say when each section happens without the aid of the chart.

Cross-curricular links

Language – telling a story through music.
Maths – noticing sections and patterns.
Art – stimulating the visual imagination through music.
Topic work– would fit with a topic on weather, seasons, transport.

'The Little Train of Caipira'

Suitable for

KS1, KS2

Aims

- To encourage the telling of a story related to a piece of music.
- To encourage the use of art work to illustrate a story connected with a piece of music.
- To give the children a greater understanding of a piece of music.

Resources

- A recording of 'The Little Train of Caipira' by Hector Villa-Lobos
- A CD player
- An art medium through which the children will be able to produce illustrations for the story contained in the music

What to do

- Explain a little about the music the children are going to hear.
- It is a piece of music that tells the story of a train journey and was written (composed) by a man from Brazil, so the story takes place in Brazil.
- Explain that it is a steam train, so at the beginning of the piece maracas and guiros are used for the train starting up.
- Let the children see and hear these instruments before they listen to the music.
- Explain that the violins in the orchestra play the tune that we hear and have a picture of a violin and/or an orchestra for the children to see.
- Explain that once the train gets going the music speeds up and the train sounds its whistle, which is played by the clarinet.
- Have a picture of a clarinet for the children to see.
- The music then changes gear as if the little train is shocked by the hill that it is going to have to pull itself up.
- The music plays the sound of the train bravely chugging up the hill and gradually managing to get going again.

- The melody is now played by all the woodwind instruments (flute, oboe, clarinet, and bassoon) and there are lots of clanking sounds from the percussion section.
- As the train draws near to the station there are warning hoots from the brass instruments and **trills** (quick alternating notes) from the woodwind instruments.
- Finally, the train begins to slow down as it goes into the station and the maracas are heard again as there is the hiss of escaping steam.
- The squeal of the brakes on the metal wheels is played by the violins using **harmonics** (placing a finger very lightly on the violin string to produce an extremely high, delicate note).
- Just as everyone is straining to hear the last squeal from the brakes, the composer puts in a loud chord from the orchestra which gives everyone a fright.
- Having discussed the story let the children listen to the piece of music.
- Don't be afraid to point out what is happening as the music plays, it is useful for the children to have regular focus points as they listen out for certain parts of the story or instruments.
- Once the children have heard the music, ask them if they could suggest a series of pictures which would tell the story and could be used for following the music.
- Either ask each child to produce a story board of pictures for the music or work as a group to produce a series of pictures which tell the story of the music.

Variations

- The leader of the group could present the music initially by having pictures of the various parts of the train journey alongside the appropriate instruments.
- The music could be put on without any previous discussion and the children have to decide what to draw appropriate to their listening of the music.

Cross-curricular links

Art – visual depiction of a piece of music.
Language – telling a story with music as the stimulus.
Science – observing and discussing how the composer uses different sounds for the various effects he requires.

Shopping for Sounds

Suitable for

KS1, KS2

Aims

- To encourage careful listening.
- To develop memory and recall.

Resources

- Room for everyone to sit in a circle
- A large selection of untuned percussion instruments and assorted sound makers – as many different kinds as possible

What to do

- Sit the children in a circle and number them from 1 up to the number in the class.
- Place all the instruments and sound makers in the middle of the circle.
- Talk about the kind of sounds you might need to shop for, e.g.:
  a tap
  a shake
  a rattle
  a ping
  a squeak
  a snort, etc.
- The first child starts and says: 'I went shopping and I bought a tap.'
- That child then chooses an instrument or sound maker on which to make a 'tap' sound.
- The rest of the class then says: 'She went shopping and bought a tap' and the child makes one 'tap' sound on their instrument.
- The second child then says: 'I went shopping and I bought a shake.'
- That child then chooses an instrument or sound maker on which to make a 'shake' sound.

- The rest of the class then says: 'He went shopping and bought a shake (the second child makes two shakes with his instrument – because he is second) and a tap' (the first child makes one tap on her instrument – because she is first).
- The third child then says: 'I went shopping and I bought a rattle.'
- That child chooses an instrument or sound maker on which to make a 'rattle' sound.
- The rest of the class then says: 'She went shopping and bought a rattle (the third child makes three rattles on her instrument – because she is third) and a shake (the second child makes two shakes on his instrument – because he is second) and a tap' (the first child makes one tap on her instrument – because she is first).
- The game continues until everyone in the circle has a sound they have bought and an instrument to play it on.
- Bear in mind that the voice is an instrument so if the sound lends itself to being vocalised more than played, e.g., a scream or 'psst', then the voice could be used instead of trying to find an appropriate instrument.
- The fact that each person has an instrument or sound maker with which to make their sound assists the children playing the game with remembering the list of sounds.

Variations

- You could try building up the shopping list without the memory aid of the instruments but this is extremely difficult.
- You could try having only the actual sound played by the instruments and not say the word for the sound.

Cross-curricular links

Language – descriptive words.
All areas – building up memory.

Entertain the Entertainer

Suitable for

KS1, KS2

Aims

- To encourage an understanding of form in music.
- To familiarise the children with a famous piece of ragtime music.
- To encourage the use of untuned percussion to accompany the music.

Resources

- A recording of Scott Joplin's ragtime piece 'The Entertainer'
- A CD player
- A copy per child of the music score that they are going to play
- The class music score written on the board

What to do

- Give the children some background information about ragtime music: Scott Joplin is probably the most famous ragtime composer and 'The Entertainer' is probably his most famous ragtime piece.
- Explain to the children that pieces of music are usually divided into sections and often a tune will be played and then repeated before a new tune is introduced.
- Go through the class music score and explain that they need to listen for the introduction then the tunes changing from sections A to B then back to A, then C followed by the introduction theme again and finally section D.
- Let the class simply listen to the piece of music and try to follow what the piece is doing as it goes along.
- It is quite helpful if the leader points out when the tunes change in case some children have difficulty recognising when it happens.
- Next divide the class into three sections: A, B and C (section D is when all three sections play together).
- Go over section A, first saying the rhythms in taa and tate and then playing them on the rhythm sticks.

- Do the same with the tambourines and then the same with the maracas and tambours.
- The children playing section C would be best to say tate taa 1, 2, to help them sort out their rhythm.
- Likewise, in section A, it may be more helpful to say 1, 2, 3, 4, tate tate taa.
- Play the recording and ask each group to play when it is their turn.
- Once the children are confident enough, they can attempt section D which is all three sections playing at the same time.

Variations

- During the learning process, the children can simply listen to the piece or have it as a backing track whilst they say their part.
- Once the instruments are added the piece could be played whilst each section in turn tries out their part.
- Obviously the more times the children hear the piece through, the more they will understand how the music is put together.

Cross-curricular links

Environmental Studies – fits with a Victorian topic as ragtime developed prior to and during Victorian times.

History – the whole history of ragtime and how it fits into the history of slavery out of which came blues and jazz music.

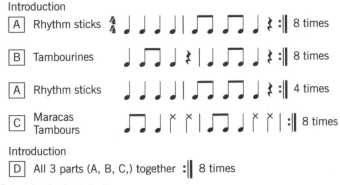

'The Entertainer' – Scott Joplin

'River Runs Red'

Suitable for

KS1, KS2

Aims

- To appreciate the style of the music.
- To learn how to feel a beat through making specific actions to accompany the music.
- To understand how composers use music to express an issue they feel strongly about.
- Perhaps lead into an art session in which the class, having explored the music, make a representation of it in a painting or drawing.

Resources

- A recording of the group Midnight Oil singing 'River Runs Red'
- A copy of the words for each member of the class
- A CD player

What to do

- Listen to the song in its entirety and ask the class to notice the long introduction, the very strong beat – how is it being played?
- Notice also the words and what they are saying.
- What pictures are they painting?
- Is there a chorus?
- It is always a good idea to have something that the children are listening for, i.e., purposeful listening.
- Obviously people listen to music simply for enjoyment, but in an activity like this it is much more meaningful for the children if it is made clear what they are listening for.
- Taking a line of the song at a time, decide what action the class are going to do – on the beat – to represent that line, e.g.:

  - *So you cut all the tall trees down*
    (a cutting motion with both hands 'chopping' each other)
  - *You poisoned the sky and the sea*
    (point with both hands upwards then downwards)

- *You've taken what's good from the ground*
  (a pulling motion with both hands as if pulling up a turnip!)
- *But you left precious little for me*
  (alternate holding both hands out in front of you and pointing to yourself)
- *You remember the flood and the fall*
  (make a wave movement with both hands then slowly push both hands downwards)
- *We remember the light on the hill*
  (use one hand to make a flashing light movement, held up high)
- *There should be enough for us all*
  (put hands out at either side then spread them out in front of you)
- *But the dollar is driving us still*
  (with alternate hands rub the thumb and two fingers together to indicate money)

- These are simply suggestions; the children will have plenty of ideas of their own.
- When it comes to the chorus, the actions should remain the same each time the chorus is sung. Suggestions are:

  - *River runs red*
    (make a river move by crossing your arms in an undulating manner)
  - *Black rain falls*
    (both hands move downwards with the fingers rippling to indicate rain)
  - *Dust in my hand*
    (alternate laying one hand on top of the other)
  - *On my bleeding hand*
    (alternate one hand pointing into the other)

- Continue and make up actions for the second verse then practise doing the actions along with the music. Suggestions for verse 2 are:
  - *So we came and conquered and found*
    (put both arms in a conquering stance, with fists raised above the head then put both hands out in front of you)
  - *Riches of commons and kings*
    (mime putting a crown on your head alternating with putting your hands on your waist)

- *Who strangled and wrestled the ground*
  (make a strangling motion with your hands and alternate with pointing to the floor)
- *But they never put back anything*
  (alternate hands pointing downwards)
- *Now I'm trapped like a dog in a cage*
  (alternate hands with fingers splayed out, put in front of your face like bars on a cage)
- *Wherever the truth is pursued*
  (slow-motion running with arms moving)
- *It must be the curse of the age*
  (alternate arms or hands making a cross action with hands being held out in front of you)
- *What's taken is never renewed*
  (three movements of both hands taking something from below and pulling it up to be held against the body, then both hands held out in front)

Variations

- Only do actions for the chorus
- Add untuned percussion instruments to the long introduction making sure they are played precisely on the beat. You could make up different combinations of instruments to accompany the introduction.

Cross-curricular links

Topic work – links with conservation, pollution, looking after the earth.
Language – how words are used to convey emotions and strong feelings.
PSHE – discussion of feelings and how music can be a useful vehicle for the expression of feelings.
Art – using music as a stimulus for art work.

'River Runs Red' – Midnight Oil
So you cut all the tall trees down
You poisoned the sky and the sea
You've taken what's good from the ground
But you left precious little for me
You remember the flood and the fall
We remember the light on the hill
There should be enough for us all
But the dollar is driving us still.

River runs red, black rain falls
Dust in my hand
River runs red, black rain falls
On my bleeding hand

So we came and conquered and found
Riches of commons and kings
Who strangled and wrestled the ground
But they never put back anything
Now I'm trapped like a dog in a cage
Wherever the truth is pursued
It must be the curse of the age
What's taken is never renewed.

'Alla Turca' Animals

Suitable for

KS1, KS2

Aims

- To encourage listening with a purpose.
- To familiarise the children with a piece of classical music.
- To encourage the use of words and singing to develop the children's understanding of the music.

Resources

- A recording of Mozart's Piano Sonata No. 11 in A major – called 'Alla Turca'
- A CD player
- A copy of the 'Alla Turca' words for each child

What to do

- The person leading this activity needs to be very familiar with both the music and the words and how the words fit to the music.
- The leader will need to have practised a lot, fitting the words to the different sections of the music.
- Play the music to the children and ask them what instruments they can hear.
- Ask them to describe the music and to notice the different sections of the music.
- The person leading the activity could then perform the whole piece with words to the children.
- Look at the words with the children.
- Start with the easiest section, which is Section 3, and say the words in time with the music they will eventually be said to.
- Each time Section 3 comes, it is repeated, so practise saying Section 3 twice.
- Now put on the music and insert the saying of Section 3 into the appropriate bit of music. (It comes in at three different places.)
- The next sections to try are Sections 1 and 2, which sometimes come twice and sometimes only once.

- Say the words first then try fitting them to the music.
- Once Sections 1, 2 and 3 have been practised, the children could perform them and the leader could put in Sections 4, 5 and 6.
- For older children, Sections 4 and 5 are quite challenging because the music is very fast, and therefore the words are very quick.
- Perhaps individual children would like the challenge of saying these sections.
- Section 6 is extremely tricky to say as it is almost impossibly fast.
- If the leader has a go at saying it, then the children could set themselves a challenge of trying to master it over time!
- Section 7 and the ending are set out to make the spaces between the words clear.
- Most children should manage to say these sections.

Variations

- For younger children, it is quite useful to make appropriate actions for Sections 1, 2 and 3.
- Actions could also be made for Section 7 and the ending.

Sections 4, 5 and 6 are too fast for any actions to be added.

Cross-curricular links

Language – articulation, the content of the words fitting to the music.
Topic work – would fit with any topic that covers animals, jungle, conservation.

Listen to the noise! Listen to the noise!   1
In the jungle animals are making lots of sounds.
Lions and monkeys, snakes and tigers.
They are moving all around.

In the jungle, they can have such fun.   2
Climbing trees or going for a run.
Chase each other, shouting to be heard.
In the air there's lots of fancy birds.

Here they come! It's the elephants, they're stamping through the jungle.   3
Such big feet! If you listen you can hear the rumbling sound.

Listen to the monkeys as they chatter in the trees and as they're climbing with 4
their knees, they're really cheeky little monkeys.
Can you listen to the monkeys as they chatter in the trees and as they're climbing
with their knees, they're really cheeky little imps.

Can you see the crocodiles? They're swimming in the water now. Be careful not
to go too near in case they try to eat you!
Can you see the crocodiles? They're swimming in the water now. Be careful not
to go too near in case they eat you up!   5

All the snkes are slithering along the branches. Up and down they go and if
they squeeze you, you would not like it all! Because you do not want to be
their lunch, they do not munch, they simply swallow everything in one big
gulp – so in you'd go – oh no!   6

Now we've seen so many different animals at play.   7
Time to go away.
It's time to leave them all alone to go to sleep and later we may peep.

ENDING
And so, we go, we've had a lovely time. Good night!

```
          1  1  2  1  2  1  3  3  4  4  5  6  5  6

       3  3  1  1  2  1  2  1  3  3  7  7  ENDING
```

Mozart Piano Sonata No.11 in A Major – 'Alla Turca'

Sing the Note then Find It

Suitable for

KS1, KS2

Aims

- To encourage the children to 'tune in' to a certain pitch and then be able to identify the note being sung.
- To develop inner hearing and relate it to a classroom tuned percussion instrument.

Resources

- A tuned percussion instrument for every two children
- Two matching beaters for each instrument

What to do

- Have a glockenspiel or xylophone set up with only two notes at first – low C and low D.
- Say beforehand which of the two notes you are going to play then play the note three times and ask the children to sing them back to you:

      Play C C C Class sings C C C
      Play D D D Class sings D D D

- After practising this several times explain that you would like someone to guess which note you are playing.
- Making sure the children cannot see which note you are playing, choose one of these notes, play it three times and ask an individual child to sing which note they think it is.
- Whichever note they sing, ask them to check by playing the note three times on their glockenspiel.
- After a relatively short time, the children will easily be able to tell if the note is C or D, so then you introduce E.
- Always ask the whole group to sing back the notes at first until everyone is sure of the notes available to choose from.

- When adding another note to choose from, take the next note up and do a lot of reinforcing before asking individuals to guess the note.
- Only move on to introducing another note when everyone is confident with the number of notes they already have.

Variations

- When there are three notes available, you could play a little melody and ask the class or an individual to sing back what they think you have played, e.g.:

   Play C D E Class sings C D E
   Play E E D Class sings E E D

- As before, practise the singing back several times before asking individuals to try and guess what is being played.
- The children could play this in pairs and take turns to be the player or the guesser.

Cross-curricular links

Language – listening skills.
PSHE – confidence building, raising self-esteem – I can do this!

Gallery of Sounds

Suitable for

KS1, KS2

Aims

- To develop listening skills
- To use listening excerpts as a stimulus for art work

Resources

- CD player
- Variety of descriptive pieces of music, e.g.:
  Tchaikovsky's 'Nutcracker Suite'
  Mussorgsky's 'Pictures at an Exhibition'
  Mendelssohn's 'Hebrides Overture'
- Paper and pens or paint

What to do

- Play an excerpt of music and ask the children to decide individually what they think the music is describing.
- Decide how many sections you want to have, e.g., four or six or eight for each piece of listening.
- Ask the children to draw a picture for each section – this can be as detailed or simple as time allows.
- After two or three excerpts, the pictures could be cut up and a partner could try to put them into the correct sequence.

Variation

- Approaching this another way, you could have already prepared a few sequences of pictures and ask the children to listen to the music and put the pictures in order according to what they hear. This should stimulate discussion about each piece of music.

Cross-curricular links

Language – descriptive language with music as the stimulus.
Topic work – choose a descriptive piece of music appropriate to the topic being studied.
Maths – sequencing.

Glossary

Accompaniment – a background part which supports the main tune.

Arco – an indication to a string player that they should use their bow to produce the sound.

Arpeggio – a set of notes which moves in small jumps often using the solfa notes doe, me, so, doe.

Ascending – moving upwards in either steps or jumps.

Beat – the pulse in music which is collected in small groups called the beats in a bar or the time signature.

Binary form – a piece of music that has two different parts to it. Often the parts are given the titles of part A and part B. Using this terminology, binary form is AB or if the sections are to be repeated AABB.

Blues scale – a variation on a major scale that allows a person to improvise above a simple 12-bar pattern. There are several different blues scales but they all use some sort of variation of the major scale that flattens (lowers slightly) the third or seventh note of the scale.

Brass – a family or set of instruments which all use valves to produce their sound.

Chord – two or more notes that are played simultaneously to harmonise.

Chord sequence – a pattern of chords.

Chorus – a part of a song which recurs between the verses.

Chromatic – the word used to describe a tuned percussion instrument that has a full set of sharp and flat bars.

Coda – a section of music to end a piece.

Compose – to make up and write music.

Conduct – to move your arms in a recognised pattern in order to guide an instrumental or singing group

Crotchet – one-beat note.

Descant – A tune that is sung or played higher than the main tune.

Descending – moving downwards in either steps or jumps.

Diatonic – the word used to describe a tuned percussion instrument that has no sharp or flat bars.

Discordant – notes that are meant to sound unpleasant when played together.

Doe – the first and last 'person' on the solfa staircase. The first and last note in a major scale (eight notes ascending or descending in a certain order). On the solfa staircase, bottom doe is always coloured red and top doe is always coloured purple. The first note of a major scale is often called the 'keynote'.

Drone – a device used in making music (often Scottish music) that involves playing two notes that are a fifth apart, e.g., C and G or F and C. Playing these notes at the same time simulates the sound of bagpipes having air blown through them.

Duet – any combination of two players or singers.

Eight-note scale – a sequence of notes that follow alphabetically from the first note, e.g., C D E F G A B C

Fa – the fourth 'person' on the solfa staircase which is always coloured pink. Fa is always one note higher than me and one note lower than so.

Fanfare – a short burst of music often played on brass instruments to announce something important happening.

Flat – a musical sign that has the effect of lowering a note by a small amount called a semitone.

Form – the patterns of tunes used to construct a piece of music.

Glockenspiel – a tuned percussion instrument that has metal bars.

Glissando – a sliding movement from one end of a glockenspiel or xylophone to the other using one beater.

Graphic score – a pictorial way of notating music.

Grid notation – a means of writing and reading music by way of a squared grid.

Harmonics – notes which are produced by playing, for instance, very lightly on a violin string and sound very high and light.

Improvisation – the art of making up music on the spot.

Instrumental – a piece of music played with instruments only in the middle of a piece of singing.

Interval – the pitch gap between two notes.

Introduction – a short section of music to begin a piece.

Key – refers to the sequence of notes from a scale that a piece of music is based on. The number of sharps or flats at the beginning of the music give an indication of the key that the music is written in.

Key signature – the number of sharps or flats written immediately after the treble clef in a piece of music.

La – the sixth 'person' on the solfa staircase which is always coloured yellow. La is always one note higher than so and one note lower than tee.

Major scale – a set of notes with a particular pattern of intervals between the notes.

Me – the third 'person' on the solfa staircase which is always coloured orange. Me is always one note higher than ray and one note lower than fa.

Melody – another name for the tune of a piece.

Middle C – the note lies in the middle of a piano or keyboard and is often the lowest note on a classroom glockenspiel or xylophone.

Minim – two-beat note

Octave – two notes that are eight steps apart. They are always the same letter name i.e. an octave E.

Off-beat note – a note that is played or sung in-between the standard beat of a piece, e.g., 1 and a 2 and a 3.

On-beat note – a note that is played or sung on one of the beats of a piece, e.g., 1 2 3 4.

Orchestra – a large group of instruments containing the four families of strings, brass, woodwind and percussion.

Ostinato – a repeating pattern of melody and/or rhythm.

Pentatonic scale – a particular scale of notes which uses five notes taken from a major scale, namely doe, ray, me, so and la.

Percussion – a family or set of instruments which are hit or struck to produce their sound.

Phrase – a small section of music, similar to the use of phrase in language.

Pitch – the highness or lowness of music. Melodies are made up of notes which vary in pitch.

Pizzicato – a technique used by string players when they pluck the strings instead of using the bow.

Pulse – the regular beat in music, similar to a human pulse.

Quavers – half-beat notes.

RAP – rhythmically accentuated poetry.

Ray – the second 'person' on the solfa staircase which is always coloured green. Ray is always next to red doe on the staircase and sounds one note higher than red doe.

Repeat sign – two vertical lines with two dots before them which indicate that the preceding music is to be played again.

Rondo – a recognised form of music where there is a main theme which recurs separated by several different themes.

Scale – a sequence of notes which follow a particular pattern.

Semibreve – a four-beat note

Semiquaver – a quarter-beat note

Semitone – the smallest gap between two notes, e.g., from F to F# is a semitone, or from B to C is a semitone.

Sharp – a musical sign that has the effect of raising a note by a small amount called a semitone.

Sixths – singing or playing notes simultaneously that are six notes apart from each other, e.g., C and A or F and D.

So – the fifth 'person' on the solfa staircase which is always coloured blue. So is always one note higher than fa and one note lower than la. The fifth note of a major scale is often called the 'dominant'.

Solfa – a method of notating music using the names doe, ray, me, fa, so, la, tee and doe.

Solfa Staircase – a visual aid to understanding and remembering the names used for notating music. Each note is illustrated as a person in a particular colour and with its own name. The notes at the bottom and the top of the staircase each have the same name: doe. This is because doe is the keynote or first note of the scale. The sequence of notes is: doe, ray, me, fa, so, la, tee, doe. The spelling of these names is altered slightly from the traditional spelling so that beginner readers can easily sound them out.

Solo – a performance for one person.

Stave – the pattern of five lines and four spaces that musical notes are written on.

Strings – a family or set of instruments which all have strings to produce their sound.

Syncopated – playing notes that are off the normal accent of the beat. The rhythm of the notes is in-between the regular beat.

Taa – the rhythmic name for a one-beat note.

Tate – the rhythmic name for two half-beat notes which are joined together.

Tee – the seventh 'person' on the solfa staircase which is always coloured brown. Tee is always one note higher than la and one note lower than purple doe.

Ternary form – a piece of music that is separated into three parts: a first section, a second section and then the first section is repeated. Ternary form is often written as A B A.

Thirds – singing or playing notes simultaneously that are three notes apart from each other, e.g., C and E or F and A.

Time signature – the two numbers that are written immediately after the key signature to indicate how many beats are in a bar for the piece of music.

Treble clef – the sign written at the beginning of a piece of music which indicates that the notes are written using the FACE and Every Good Boy Deserves Football pattern of lines and spaces.

Tremolo – a technique for producing a continuous sound which involves using rapidly alternating beaters on a glockenspiel or xylophone.

Trill – a repeated pattern of playing one note and the note either above or below it.

Tuned percussion – a percussion instrument that is capable of playing a tune, i.e., glockenspiel or xylophone.

Turnabout beaters – using a beater in each hand and playing the glockenspiel or xylophone with each beater in turn or 'turnabout'.

Unison – everyone playing or singing the same part together.

Untuned percussion – a percussion instrument that is capable of playing a rhythm but not a melody, i.e., tambourine or triangle.

Verse – part of a song which is different each time and often has a recurring chorus between every appearance.

Woodwind – a family or set of instruments which all require blowing and often a reed to produce their sound.

Xylophone – a tuned percussion instrument that has wooden bars.

Instruments of the Orchestra

There are four families of instruments in an orchestra:

Strings
Brass
Woodwind
Percussion

String family

Violin, viola, cello and double bass are the usual string intruments in an orchestra. Some orchestra include the harp in the string section but others put in the percussion section.

Brass family

Trumpet, trombone, french horn and tuba are the usual brass instruments in an orchestra.

Woodwind family

Flute, oboe, clarinet and bassoon are the usual woodwind instruments in an orchestra. A piccolo is often used and occasionally a cor anglais. The bass clarinet and double bassoon are needed for some pieces.

Percussion family

There are numerous instruments in this section, basically anything that can be struck or hit. All orchestral percussion sections would have timpani/kettle drums, snare drum, cymbals, bass drum, glockenspiel/xylophone, tambourine, woodblocks, triangle, maracas, sleigh bells. There are many instruments that may be required for certain pieces of music including castanets, whip, celesta, tamtam and tubular bells.

Sources for songs

This is simply a selction of the song sources I use most frequently. Obviously, it is certainly not an exhaustive list and is merely provided as a starting point for finding songs to fit your own individual needs.

A & C Black – many and varied songbooks including –

Me – songs for 4–7 year olds
Tom Thumb's Musical Maths – Helen McGregor
Michael Finigan, Tap Your Chinigin – Sue Nicholls
Bingo Lingo – Helen McGregor
Bobby Shaftoe, Clap Your Hands – Sue Nicholls
Sing a Story – Graham Westcott
www.acblack.com

Eileen Diamond – many and varied songbooks –
www.musicroom.com

Fischy Music – Angry Hotel Man, Build Up, Down to Earth, It's a Noisy World, Just Imagine, Something Fischy, These Are Our Emotions – all songs written by Stephen Fischbacher and superb for assembly/PSE situations –
www.fischy.com

Golden Apple – many and varied songbooks –
www.musicsales.com

I Sing, You Sing – Sally K. Albrecht and Jay Althouse – echo songs to develop call and response.
www.alfredpub.com/chorhome.html

Jan Holdstock – many and varied songbooks
www.musicroom.com

Junior Songscape KS1–2 – Lin Marsh
Junior Songscape KS1–2, Earth, Sea and Sky – Lin Marsh
www.fabermusic.com

Kids Music Education – many songbooks with CDs including –

Swing Thing
Feeling the Beat
Echo Fred
Pukeko Stomp
Jump, Jive and Improvise
You've Got to Clap

all by Janet Channon and Wendy Jensen
www.KidsMusicEducation.com

Notable Songs Limited – currently 25 topic-related songpacks – all written by Donna Minto – titles are:
Vikings, School, Food, Clothes, Night, Space, Cinderella, Goldilocks, Jack and the Beanstalk, Sleeping Beauty, People Who Help Us, Dinosaurs, Christmas, Toys, Colours, Transport, Weather, Animals, Ancient Egypt, Praise Songs for Assembly, Growing and Us, Do You Know ...?, People and Places, Romans and Celts, Energy.
www.notablesongs.co.uk

Out of the Ark Music – many and varied songbooks – all written by Mark and Helen Johnson
www.outoftheark.com

Sing for Pleasure, Junior Song Book Pack
www.singforpleasure.org.uk

Singing Sherlock – books 1, 2, 3, 4 – Val Whitlock and Shirley Court
www.boosey.com

Sixty Sizzling Songs – Sarah Watts – also *Red Hot Dots* by Sarah Watts
www.kevinmayhew.com

Traditional Scottish Songs and Music – Katherine Campbell and Ewan McVicar
www.leckieandleckie.co.uk

Classroom Gems

nnovative resources, inspiring creativity across the school curriculum

Designed with busy teachers in mind, the Classroom Gems series draws together an extensive selection of practical, tried-and-tested, off-the-shelf ideas, games and activities, guaranteed to transform any lesson or classroom in an instant.

2008 Paperback 336pp
ISBN: 9781405873925

© 2008 Paperback 312pp
ISBN: 9781405859455

© 2009 Paperback 216pp
ISBN: 9781408220382

© 2009 Paperback 232pp
ISBN: 9781408225578

2009 Paperback 384pp
ISBN: 9781408224359

© 2009 Paperback 392pp
ISBN: 9781408223208

© 2009 Paperback 320pp
ISBN: 9781408228098

© 2009 Paperback 352pp
ISBN: 9781408223291

2009 Paperback 192pp
ISBN: 9781408225608

'Easily navigable, allowing teachers to choose the right activity quickly and easily, these invaluable resources are guaranteed to save time and are a must-have tool to plan, prepare and deliver first-rate lessons'